The

Hugh Montefiore was born in Paddington in 1920 and educated at Rugby and St John's College, Oxford, of which he became an Honorary Fellow in 1981. Born a Jew, he was converted to Christianity at the age of sixteen.

After the Second World War, during which he served with the Royal Bucks Yeomanry, he trained for the ministry and was ordained a priest of the Church of England in 1950. After a curacy at Jesmond, Newcastle, he began a distinguished academic career as Chaplain, Tutor and finally Vice Principal of Westcott House, Cambridge, and then Examining Chaplain to four bishops 1953–70. He returned to Cambridge in 1954 to become successively Fellow and Dean of Gonville and Caius College (1954–63), Lecturer in New Testament, University of Cambridge (1959–63), and Vicar of Great St Mary's (1963–70).

In 1970 Hugh Montefiore became Bishop Suffragan of Kingston upon Thames, and in 1978 Bishop of Birmingham. He officially retired in 1987, but has continued his active interest in many things, including the writing of books, and his weekly column in *The Church Times*.

The Womb and the Tomb

by

Hugh Montefiore

Fount

An Imprint of HarperCollins*Publishers*

First published in Great Britain
in 1992 by Fount Paperbacks

Fount Paperbacks is an imprint of
HarperCollinsReligious
Part of HarperCollins*Publishers*
77–85 Fulham Palace Road, London W6 8JB

Typeset by Medcalf Type Ltd, Bicester, Oxon

Printed and bound in Great Britain by
HarperCollinsManufacturing, Glasgow

A catalogue record for this book is
available from the British Library

Contents

Introduction

Was Jesus the child of a virgin? Was he raised physically from the dead? These are the two questions which this book seeks to investigate. They no longer make screaming headlines as they did a few years ago when Dr David Jenkins raised them at the time of his nomination as Bishop of Durham. But they are still questions which worry many Christians, either because they are shocked that other Christians should question them, or because they find them difficult to accept themselves. I have to admit that they have worried me throughout my active ministry. Here in this book I attempt a scrupulously fair discussion of both beliefs (although I may well not have succeeded in this aim), in the hope that this will not only help people who want to find out more about these matters, but may also assist those who have definite views to respect the views of those who differ from them. I do not disclose my own views until the Epilogue at the end of the book.

In the recent past the debate has usually been conducted at a superficial level. Those in favour have been dubbed 'conventional Christians' as though that were something about which to be ashamed, and those against have been regarded as 'radicals', as though they were hardly Christians at all. Here I have tried to set out the arguments of both sides in a reasoned way which cuts across such facile judgements. There will inevitably be some who say that both the 'Virgin Birth' and the physical Resurrection of Jesus would be so miraculous and so unprecedented as to be absolutely incredible in today's modern world; but further reflection will show that the Incarnation itself is far more miraculous and far more unprecedented than any beliefs about how it began or ended. There will be others who say that the very fact that the 'Virgin Birth' and the Resurrection are found in the Scriptures and in the creeds is a sufficient guarantee of their truth; and that this is the end of the matter. Again, a little further thought will show that the Scriptures need to be interpreted, and apparent inconsistencies do need to be explained and ironed out, and that it is generally agreed that not all statements in the Creed are to be accepted literally. Again, there are those who say that because the Church has from its very early days believed in the 'Virgin Birth' and the empty tomb (and has shown great reverence to the Blessed Virgin Mary as the mother of Jesus), these two beliefs should not be questioned; but again, a little further thought will show that, if the Church relies solely on its own authority for affirming what it believes to be true, without any other supporting evidence, it is unlikely to commend itself to those who do not accept its absolute authority. What is needed is a way of affirming the authority of Scripture and tradition which does justice to our God-given powers of reason.

I have aimed in this book at evaluating the literary evidence about the 'Virgin Birth' and the empty tomb, as well as examining the doctrinal implications of these beliefs and the illumination (if any) that modern science can throw on the nature of these miracles. These are complex matters which deserve continuing investigation and reflection. I have tried to set out the arguments and to conduct the debate in a scholarly way; but this is not an academic study, so I have avoided learned references and cut down footnotes to a minimum. In this way I hope that, without sacrificing rigour of thought or omitting important considerations, I can make accessible to the ordinary reader what underlies recent controversy on these matters.

I am a member of the Church of England, and until my retirement I was a diocesan bishop, so my treatment of these matters has been coloured by recent controversy within that Church. But I am aware that they have also surfaced in other Churches (for example in the Church of Scotland, where a summary of faith has been proposed which omits mention of the 'Virgin Birth' of Jesus). These beliefs are of concern to all Christians, and I hope therefore that this book may be of interest to members of other Churches as well as my own.

In 1986 there was published a pamphlet entitled *The Nature of Christian Belief* with the subtitle *A Statement and Exposition by the House of Bishops of the General Synod of the Church of England*, in the aftermath of the furore caused by the remarks of Dr David Jenkins, Bishop of Durham, on these matters. This pamphlet of the bishops makes a convenient jumping off point for this enquiry. It was a consensus document rather than an individual viewpoint. In the short Statement at the beginning of the booklet, the bishops confirmed their faith in the Resurrection of Christ as an objective reality, as they did also in the full divinity of Christ. However, in dealing with the 'Virgin Birth' and the physical Resurrection of Jesus their language was different. Here there is no mention of the personal beliefs of the bishops. They simply upheld these beliefs 'as expressing the faith of the Church of England', which is not the same thing at all. The relevant paragraphs of their statement are as follows:

(3) As regards belief that Christ's tomb was empty on the first Easter Day, we acknowledge and uphold this as expressing the faith of the Church of England and as affirming that in the resurrection the material order is redeemed, and the fulness of human nature, bodily, mental and spiritual, is glorified for eternity.
(5) As regards the Virginal Conception of Our Lord, we acknowledge and uphold belief in this as expressing the faith of the Church of England, and as affirming that in Christ God has taken the initiative for our salvation by uniting with himself our human nature, so bringing to birth a new humanity.[1]

The bishops did not affirm that these are the *only* ways of affirming the faith of the Church of England, because not all of them would have agreed with that. Nor did they say that they were all united in holding these beliefs, because they weren't. They upheld these beliefs in so far as they express the official faith of the Church. (In fact the bishops had affirmed them as 'expressing part of the faith of the Church'. The unauthorized omission of the phrase 'part of' was no doubt made in order to tidy up the English, but it is not what the bishops actually agreed.)

The empty tomb and the 'Virgin Birth' do certainly express part of the official faith of the Church, although personally I am doubtful whether the living faith of today's Church can be expressed in its wholeness by means of theological formularies. When considering the theological problems of Godhead and manhood which are involved either at the beginning of the Incarnation or at the end of the earthly life of the Son of God, we are dealing with mysteries beyond our understanding.

I have to admit that I regarded the Exposition of both the 'Virgin Birth' and the physical Resurrection of Jesus which accompanied the bishops' Statement as inadequate. But I did not want to deny what it contained. It distinguished theological exploration from the corporate teaching of the Church, but it was still able to affirm that 'there can be a proper diversity in the understanding and expression of the Christian faith'. At a difficult time for the Church of England, when it was necessary for its bishops to show solidarity, it was better for an individual bishop to keep his counsel. And so like all the other bishops, I signed it, albeit in my case with reservations. But it seems appropriate to return again to the subject now that I have more time to do so in retirement, and after the mud stirred up by the controversy some six years earlier has settled.

This book is the result.

Part I

Chapter 1

The Virgin Birth

The two sections of this book, the first on the 'Virgin Birth' and the second on the physical Resurrection of Jesus, appear at first sight to be quite separate. But on closer inspection there is a genuine connection between them. They both concern the assumption of humanity by God in Christ and the mystery of the union of human and divine in his person. The one relates to the beginning of the Incarnation, and the other to its ending.

Christians believe that Jesus was the incarnate Son of God, not in the sense that God the Father was literally the father of the man Jesus, but in the sense that the eternal Son of God assumed humanity, so that the Word became flesh and dwelt among us, and in the one person Jesus Christ there were united both divine and human nature. This fundamental Christian conviction is encapsulated in the belief that Jesus was conceived not like the rest of mankind who all have both a human father and a human mother, but in a miraculous way which did not require male co-operation. This is often described as the 'Virgin Birth', but in fact it ought to be clearly distinguished from it. The Virgin Birth stictly speaking refers to the belief which arose very early in the life of the Church and which was accepted by many early Fathers, that the actual process of Jesus' birth was so miraculous that it left Mary intact as a virgin with her hymen unruptured. This does not form part of the official faith of the Church, and I will not comment further upon it. But so as to leave no room for ambiguity, I will from now on use the phrase Virginal Conception rather than 'Virgin Birth' in referring to the belief that Jesus was born without the agency of a human father.

The enquiry will take us into very intimate areas of life into which it is appropriate to enter only with modesty and discretion. For example, women have from time to time alleged they have conceived as virgins; but if the birth has already taken place, proof or disproof is impossible even after physical examination, except perhaps by means of the modern technique of 'genetic fingerprinting'. Even if the birth has not yet taken place, and the woman is found to be still a virgin, this would not necessarily rule out the possibility of a normal conception. However, we are considering a situation utterly different from these, in which a young woman is said to have become pregnant as a result of divine not human intervention. The event is said to have taken place nearly two thousand years ago. The evidence must be very second hand. As the birth of the child took place some time before the date of the first written evidence about it, enquiry will be still more difficult. But not impossible.

It is distasteful to conduct an inquiry into such an intimate area of life; but controversy has unfortunately made it necessary. No dishonour of any kind is intended to the mother of Jesus. This needs to be said because in an earlier book I had occasion to take a critical look at the beliefs about Mary which are required from members of the Roman Catholic Church, as a result of which I was alleged to be 'making a case against Mary'.[2] That is very far from my intention. Indeed I venerate Mary, and I like to invoke her prayers more than those of any of the saints. As I wrote in answering this allegation, 'She was chosen for the most honoured role that I can imagine, to bear in her womb the Son of God. Further, she had the prime responsibility for the nurture and upbringing of Jesus, so that Christ's human nature was deeply influenced by her at its most formative stage. I find it hard to see how anyone can love and worship Christ without venerating his Mother'.

I think that it needs to be said at the outset that, however important the historicity of the Virginal Conception may seem to Christians, it does not appear to have had any importance for Jesus himself, to judge from the evidence of the gospels. He never himself laid claim to it. He did not refer to its possibility. It is possible, of course, that Jesus did speak of it, and that his words were not remembered or reported. 'There are also many other things that Jesus did, the which, if they should be written every one, I suppose that even the world itself could not contain the books that should be written' (John 21:25). If that were true of Jesus' actions, it would have been even more true of Jesus' words. Perhaps then he did speak of it; but, if so, it is very odd that such words find no echo in the gospels.

If Jesus did know about it, it seems safe to assume that he did not rate it to be very important. Today there are those who regard it as proof of Jesus' divine authority. If we look at the evidence of the gospels, we find that Jesus could be very elusive about the source of his authority (Mark 11:43), but none the less he established it in various ways. He appealed to the Scriptures. He appealed to his own mighty works. He appealed to the witness of the Holy Spirit. But he never appealed to his Virginal Conception.

If the Virginal Conception is a historical fact, his mother must have known about it better than anyone else could possibly have done. If so, she seems to have withheld this knowledge from her son, and yet to have told her story to the sources which lie behind St Matthew's and St Luke's gospels. There may be good reasons for her acting in this way; but it is not very easy to imagine what these could be. Perhaps modesty prevented her from telling her own son; but in her old age, after the death of Jesus, she felt that the truth must be made known.

The truth of the Virginal Conception as a historical event cannot be decided on such speculative grounds as these. It is necessary to examine the actual evidence, such as it is, both for and against the Virginal Conception. We shall begin by looking at the gospels, and naturally we start by examining the earliest of the four.

Chapter 2
St Mark's Gospel

It is generally agreed that St Mark's gospel was written before St Matthew's and St Luke's gospels, the other two 'synoptic' gospels. (There are some who think that it is an abbreviation of an earlier St Matthew's gospel, but they are in the minority of scholars.) There is inevitably disagreement among critics about the date when it was first published. Most people think that this took place after the Fall of Jerusalem in AD 70, some forty years after the death of Jesus and seventy years after his conception; but there are some influential scholars who believe that it was written at least a decade earlier than that.

St Mark's gospel contains no mention of the Virginal Conception; but this is not surprising when we realize that it also contains no mention of Jesus' birth or childhood. So the omission cannot by itself be taken in any way to deny his Virginal Conception. For the author of St Mark's gospel, the good news of the gospel begins not with the Virginal Conception of Mary, but with the public ministry of John the Baptist. 'The beginning of the Gospel of Jesus Christ the Son of God' is how it starts, and then it continues in the very next verse: 'As it is written in the prophet, Behold I send my messenger before my face . . .', quoting an Old Testament passage which is applied to the coming of the Baptist. In other words, the author of St Mark's gospel appears not to see the beginning of the gospel at the conception of Jesus or at his birth, but some thirty years later when John the Baptist baptized Jesus in the river Jordan, and 'he saw the heavens opened, and the Spirit like a dove descending upon him and there came a voice from heaven, saying ''Thou art my beloved Son'' in whom I am well pleased' (Mark 1:10f.).

The explanation why there is no account in St Mark's gospel of Jesus' life prior to his baptism could be that no details were available to its author; but it does not appear that he considered that anything important was missing from his gospel if he began with so confident an opening. Some later theologians in the second century believed that Jesus was conceived in the normal way, and lived as an ordinary person until his baptism, when he was 'adopted' by God as his son. The divine voice at his baptism, however, does not imply that Jesus was at that point adopted as the Son of God, but that the truth about his sonship was then made known. The Church condemned what is called 'adoptionism' as heretical. It is unlikely that such views were held by the author of St Mark's gospel. It seems more likely that he never considered the mode by which Jesus was conceived.

The 'Brethren of the Lord'

St Mark's gospel mentions Jesus' brothers. 'And they said unto him, Behold, thy mother and thy brethren without seek for thee. And he answered them saying, Who is my mother or my brethren? And he looked round about them which sat about him, and said, Behold my mother and my brethren' (Mark 3:32ff.). Again, when Jesus came to his home town of Nazareth, the people exclaimed, according to St Mark's gospel: 'Is not this the carpenter, the son of Mary, the brother of James, and Joses, and of Juda, and Simon? and are not his sisters here with us?' (Mark 6:3; cf. Matthew 13:55). Paul also referred to James as 'the Lord's brother' in Galatians 1:19. The Greek word for brother is *adelphos*, but it can also mean cousin. Jerome, who translated the Bible into Latin, insisted that this was its meaning in these passages, thus enabling him to retain his belief in the perpetual virginity of Mary, in opposition to Helvidius who held that the word here has the normal meaning of brother. A mediating position was held by Epiphanius, who held that the brothers and sisters in these passages were step-brothers and step-sisters, the children of

Joseph by an earlier marriage, before he was widowed and later wedded Mary.

The classic exposition of this subject was written by Bishop John Lightfoot of Durham[3] in the last century. He dismissed Jerome's theory on the ground that the word *adelphos* normally means brother (and indeed there is a perfectly good word *anepsios* to designate a cousin). The word 'first born', which is used of Jesus, does not necessarily imply that there were any younger children. Lightfoot preferred Epiphanius's theory of Joseph's children by an earlier marriage on the grounds that Jesus, when dying on the Cross, would never have given his mother to the apostle John if he had four other surviving brothers to look after her. He did not seem to consider whether it would have been appropriate to do this if, as he supposed, there were four surviving step-brothers; nor did he consider the possibility that the gift of his mother to John has a symbolic meaning rather than a historical basis.

It is certainly reasonable to assume that, by the time of Jesus' death, Mary had been widowed. Joseph disappears from the gospel narratives after Jesus has reached the age of thirteen, while his mother appears again not infrequently; and it is reasonable to assume that the explanation is that Joseph had died shortly after Jesus came of age. This of course does not prove that Joseph was a widower from a previous marriage (with surviving children) at the time when he took Mary to wife; but, on the assumption that Joseph died early because he was older than Mary, it is probable, since Jewish men were supposed to have married and produced a son by the age of 19. There is further evidence to be considered which increases this probability.

'Jesus Son of Mary'

In the passage which has been quoted above, Jesus is called 'the carpenter, the son of Mary' (Mark 6:3). However, in biblical times people were described as being the sons of their father, not their mother. 'Jesus ben Joseph' is what we would expect, if Joseph was his actual father, or believed to have been his father. On the other hand, if a child was born to a woman who had no husband, then of course he would be known as the son of his mother. The phrase 'son of Mary' might therefore be understood to imply that Jesus was illegitimate. The other two synoptic gospels seem to realize the awkwardness of the phrase, because they do not use it. Matthew has 'Is not his mother called Mary?' (Matthew 13:55), while in Luke there is a different version of Jesus' visit to Nazareth which does not mention Mary at all (Luke 4:16ff.).

Some have suggested that Jesus was called 'son of Mary' because Joseph had died; but Jewish sources give no confirmation of such usage. Others have suggested that the author of St Mark's gospel realized that the phrase conveys a hint that Jesus was the child of an illegitimate union, but that he retained the phrase, however demeaning it might seem, because he knew about the Virginal Conception and so he thought it was appropriate because Jesus had no human father. This seems very unlikely. The passage contains no slur either on Jesus or on his mother. All that the story records is that Jesus and his whole family were well known to the townsfolk of Nazareth.

What then is the explanation of the phrase? The people of Nazareth seem to have made a distinction between Jesus and his brothers and sisters, and at the same time they affirmed their kinship. This relationship is best explained if they were known to be his step-brothers and step-sisters who shared the same father, but not the same mother. In such a case, it would have made sense to describe Jesus as 'son of Mary' to distinguish him from the rest of the family who had another mother whose name is unknown to us. So we can find some support from the phrase 'Son of Mary' for the so called 'Epiphanian' explanation of Jesus' kinsfolk. The use of this phrase cannot be properly used to prove either that Jesus was virginally conceived, or that he was the child of an illegitimate union. It simply refers to the fact that Jesus was believed to be the offspring not of Joseph's first marriage but of his later marriage to Mary.

'Out of His Mind'

St Mark's gospel tells us that, soon after Jesus had begun his public ministry, a vast crowd gathered from all parts and he had to get into a boat in order to protect himself from being thronged by the multitude. He healed many and exorcized others; and so great were the demands made upon him that he commissioned the Twelve to be with him and to proclaim the Good News (Mark 3:7–19). The pressure of the crowd was such that he had to retreat into the house at Capernaum. This reached the ears of 'those round about him' – and they must have included his family – and they concluded that he was out of his mind (Mark 3:21). They set out (presumably from his home town of Nazareth) to lay hold of him. A few verses later we are told that 'his brethren and his mother, standing without, sent for him, calling him' (Mark 3:31).

It would seem therefore that his own family, including his mother, thought that he was out of his mind. Some, however, have tried to hold that 'those around about him' and 'his brethren and his mother' are different sets of people, and that the fact that the former believed that he was out of his mind, and that his mother and his brethren later arrived to fetch him away, are quite unconnected, because they are separated by an incident in the text of St Mark's gospel. If however 'those around about him' set out from Nazareth to take him away because they thought he was mad, it would have taken them some time to get to Capernaum, and so it would have been likely that some incident intervened between the two. Why else would members of his family have wanted to call him away from his public ministry unless they believed that he was beside himself?

We are specifically told that the members of his family included his mother. Why should she have joined with them, if she knew in her heart that some thirty years earlier God had chosen her to be the mother of the incarnate Son of God through a Virginal Conception? Should she not have expected her son, with such an origin, to perform marvellous healings, to cast out evil spirits, and to attract vast crowds? Should she have been surprised that he commissioned twelve people to be with him and to help him proclaim his good news to the people? It is easy to understand why his brothers and sisters, who had been brought up alongside him and who did not know of his miraculous origin, thought that he had gone out of his mind. But if the Virginal Conception is a historical fact, a different explanation is needed in the case of his mother, who would have known only too well about his origins.

It is interesting that both St Matthew's and St Luke's gospels omit this particular verse from St Mark's gospel. This was probably done out of reverence for Jesus, because their authors did not wish to disclose that anyone thought that he was out of his mind. There is likely to be a further reason for their omission. They both record the Virginal Conception of Jesus, and they would have realized the difficulty of his mother, if she knew of his divine origin, believing that he was out of his mind.

It is not very easy to find a convincing explanation for Mary's behaviour if the Virginal Conception is a historical fact. Perhaps she wished to keep his origin a secret, and so she went along with the rest of the family. Perhaps she had a very conventional idea of the way in which the Messiah would behave, and found Jesus' behaviour inappropriate. Later John the Baptist, when he was in prison, had doubts about Jesus' public ministry and sent to assure himself that he was indeed the Messiah. It is possible that Mary's doubts were such that she was swept along by her family's conviction that he was beside himself, and so went to Capernaum with them to fetch him away.

Chapter 3
St Matthew's Gospel

Matthew's Genealogy

St Matthew's gospel, unlike St Mark's gospel, does refer to the Virginal Conception of Jesus, but it opens not with an account of his divine origins but with a record of his human forebears in the form of a genealogy. This is arranged in three groups of 14 generations from Abraham to Jesus, a Jewish literary form which helped people to memorize its contents. It is somewhat artificial because, in order to keep it down to fourteen generations, there have to be some gaps in the genealogy. It is said that it was kept to this number because the Hebrew word for David has the value of fourteen when reckoned numerologically according to the conventions of those times.

There are some remarkable features. The genealogy (which is different from the one in St Luke's gospel) does not mention the Virginal Conception, although, as we have already noticed, this is mentioned later in his gospel. The reason why it is not included here is that the genealogy is only concerned with showing that Jesus was descended from David, and that Jesus was entitled to call himself 'son of David'. (There were of course many others in Jesus' day who claimed to be descended from David.) The Greek word 'begat' is used in tracing his lineage, but this word in Hebrew can designate a legal heir rather than physical descent. The genealogy seems to have been compiled not by the Evangelist himself, but in circles which did not know about the Virginal Conception.

Another remarkable characteristic of this genealogy is that it includes five women. This was most unusual, and must have had a special purpose. This purpose becomes clearer when the identities of the five women are examined. They are Tamar, Rahab, Ruth, Bathsheba and Mary. Of the four besides Mary, only one of them was respectable, Ruth, David's great grandmother; but she was a Moabitess, a Gentile, an odd inclusion in a Jewish genealogy, showing how divine providence works in unexpected ways. Of the other three, Tamar committed adultery with her father-in-law (Genesis 38:15f.) although he pronounced her more just than himself. Rahab was a harlot by profession (Joshua 2:1), although she was considered justified by her good works (James 2:25). Bathsheba, the wife of Uriah the Hittite, committed adultery with David who later married her (2 Samuel 11:3), and she bore him their son Solomon. Presumably these women were all included to show that God's providence was at work despite sexual irregularity or racial admixture. The question has to be asked: why should the compiler of St Matthew's genealogy have deliberately included these women when there was no need for him to do so, and added also the name of Mary? A genealogy is hardly the place for a general demonstration of divine providence overruling the sexual weaknesses of men and women. It is possible that Mary's name was included to show the unexpected nature of God's choice of a young unknown girl to be the mother of the Messiah; but it is impossible to overlook the possibility that the inclusion of these names was intended to justify some kind of irregularity in the case of Mary and Joseph.

A third point to be noticed about St Matthew's genealogy concerns its ending. From the way in which the rest of it is structured, we would expect it to read: 'And Jacob begat Joseph and Joseph begat Jesus'. Something very like this is found in the Old Syriac version, which reads: 'Joseph, to whom was betrothed Mary the virgin, begat Jesus who is called the Messiah'. This translation however is not to be dated before AD 200. On the whole it is best not to regard the Old Syriac ending as the original form of the genealogy, because it is difficult to show how other readings developed from it; but it is easy to show how all the variants came into being from the best attested reading, which runs: 'And Jacob begat Joseph the husband of Mary, of whom was born Jesus who is called Christ' (Matthew 1:16). This must have seemed ambiguous to some scribes, as there are several variants to the effect that Mary was still a virgin and espoused to Joseph when she bore her son. The received text can certainly be understood in this sense, but unless the Virginal Conception were known independently, it would be natural to assume from the passage that Jesus was the natural son of a marriage between Joseph and Mary.

If Joseph was not Jesus' real father, what would have been the point of tracing his descent through Joseph? Since Joseph did marry Mary, legally speaking Jesus, like any child of the marriage, was Joseph's son, whether Joseph begat him or not. The genealogy demonstrates that, legally speaking, Jesus could trace a royal descent from King David (although Jesus did not explicitly claim this for himself). The thought of legal succession was probably in the mind of the author of St Matthew's gospel, and that was why he included the genealogy. But what of the compiler of the genealogy? It is possible that he knew that Jesus was legally Joseph's son, but that there had been some irregularity over his parents' marriage. This irregularity would have been apparent from the simple fact that Jesus was born less than nine months after the marriage took place, which leaves open the question of paternity. It seems hardly likely that the compiler himself knew about the Virginal Conception because in that case he would have been unlikely to include in it Tamar, Rahab and Bathsheba.

The Birth of Jesus According to St Matthew's Gospel

St Matthew begins his account of Jesus' birth with the statement that Mary became pregnant when she was espoused to Joseph 'before they came together'. According to Jewish law, betrothal was a legal bond which could not be informally abrogated. The usual length of betrothal was a year. Originally it included the payment of a bride price under the terms of the marriage contract; but around 70 BC this requirement was modified. Only a nominal token payment was then required under the contract agreed between the man and his betrothed's father at the time of the betrothal. Betrothal itself constituted a 'future option' to marry, and prevented the betrothed from marrying anyone else, and infidelity on her part was treated as adultery. If a man decided to terminate a betrothal, he had to give the woman a writ (*get*) which gave her back her freedom, and he also had to pay a fine to her father. A woman was regarded as a widow if her betrothed died, whether he had 'taken' her to his house (and so begun the marriage) or not. Betrothal constituted a bond which prevented other members of the two families of the betrothed from intermarrying within the prohibited degrees. So, apart from actual cohabitation, a betrothed couple were to all intents and purposes legally married. The marriage itself took place when the bride was taken to her husband's house; and the occasion of course was celebrated with a marriage feast.

Later, however, there was a further relaxation of the rules of betrothal on account of widespread poverty. Couples could not marry because the man could not afford to set up house. According to Finkelstein:

Much hardship must have been required for the early Judaean to substitute for the tradition of taking the wife to the husband's home the inverse tradition of accepting the husband in the wife's family. We may be sure that it was not done in the 'best' families. Where it was done, the woman was regarded as not properly married; she remained betrothed (*arusah*) until her husband could take her to a house of his own. The law however taking cognizance of the customary facts, says, 'He who sits at his father-in-law's house in Judaea, cannot after marriage charge his wife with the loss of virginity, for they are frequently together in private'. The spread of this habit made even the more traditional and respectable relax in their rigour. Hence in Judaea the betrothed were allowed to remain together 'for at times they were brought into the nuptial chamber in order that his heart might be attracted to her'. This was particularly reasonable because the husband and wife were of mature age. In Galilee, however, such pre-marital privacy was considered unseemly.[4]

Clearly it was irregular for pregnancy to take place during the period of betrothal, although it was not a serious misdemeanour for which Jewish law prescribed a penalty. The tradition of Judaea, from which Joseph, as a member of the house of David, must originally have come, was more relaxed in these matters than Galilee. The story of the Virginal Conception may be based on historical fact; but if it is not, it is clear that intimacy could have taken place between Joseph and Mary when they were betrothed but before he took her to his own house. This explanation would account for some of the strangenesses in the Matthean genealogy. On the other hand, if Joseph was a widower when he married Mary, he would have had a house to which to take Mary, and so he would not have been living in Mary's house prior to his marriage. This makes such an explanation less probable.

In any case, it is explicitly denied in St Matthew's gospel. Mary was found to be pregnant, and Joseph, knowing that he was not the father of Mary's child, naturally assumed that Mary had misconducted herself with someone else. Although it is doubtful whether the Jews possessed the death sentence under Roman rule, none the less under Jewish law the penalty for such misconduct was death. We are told that, so as not to expose Mary to public shame (and to whatever penalty might be exacted) Joseph determined to 'divorce' her in a way which would not cause trouble. But in reality there was no way in which he could terminate the betrothal by informal mutual agreement: a *get* was required. Even if Joseph had been able to break it off without a *get*, it is hard to see how a scandal could have been avoided. If he had not taken Mary to his house and married her, she would have become a 'single parent', and would have been publicly disgraced in Nazareth. If it were thought that Joseph had 'divorced' her after fathering her child, he would have brought a scandal on himself. In a small community it would have been impossible to keep these matters secret without causing a scandal of some kind.

Virgin Births: A New Interpretation?

According to Jewish tradition, as the Jewish scholar Geza Vermes has recently pointed out, virginity could be a word used to describe the state of a young girl before the onset of menstruation.[5] The marriage of minors was not unknown, and of course in such cases cohabitation took place. If conception took place on the occasion of the girl's first ovulation, a child could be born of the marriage before menstruation had taken place. Such births were known as 'virgin births'. The Roman Catholic scholar Rosemary Radford Reuther has endorsed this suggestion: 'The young Mary might have been thought of as a girl who is betrothed at an age too early to be fertile (a not uncommon practice at this time) and who conceives before menstruation gives the first evidence of her fertility. Rabbinic writings refer to such births as "virgin births".'[6] However, this explanation assumes that Mary married at a very tender age indeed, for which there is no evidence whatsoever, and this may be thought improbable if Joseph was already a widower when he married her. This explanation also assumes that Joseph was the father, which the author of St Matthew's gospel is at pains to point out was not the case. It is difficult to see how this kind of 'virgin birth' could have given rise to the belief that Jesus had no human father.

Dreams

According to St Matthew's gospel, Joseph was warned in a dream not to divorce his betrothed, but to take her to wife, because 'that which is conceived in her is of the Holy Ghost'. He was told that she would bear a son, and that he must name him Jesus because he would save his people from their sins. This is not the only occasion in the Matthean birth stories on which God communicates by means of a dream. The Magi were warned by a dream not to return to Herod (Matthew 2:12). Joseph was told in a dream to go down to Egypt, and in another dream to return (Matthew 2:13, 19). Later on in the gospel, Pilate's wife asks her husband not to take further proceedings against Jesus because she has been warned by a dream (Matthew 27:19). Dreams in those days were accepted as a means of divine communication with mortals, but none the less St Matthew alone of the four evangelists records them as such. This may well suggest that the Evangelist himself put into writing the story of Joseph's warning by a dream; and without this dream, the whole Matthean story of the Virginal Conception collapses. But there is no proof that this was the case: it is not impossible that Joseph really was warned in this way.

The Meaning Behind the Matthean Account

If St Matthew's account of Jesus' Virginal Conception were not supplemented by the Lucan stories, they would seem rather inadequate as an explanation of Jesus' origins. The story in St Matthew's gospel is short and bare. It hardly stands on its own. The Virginal Conception by its nature is something which would concern a woman, but the tale is told in St Matthew's gospel entirely from a man's point of view. Joseph is addressed as 'Joseph, son of David' to emphasize his Davidic descent. He was told in a dream not to divorce his betrothed. He was told how he should name the child when it was born. He immediately obeyed the orders he received in his dream, took his betrothed to his house, but had no marital relations with her until the child was born. (Those who believe in the perpetual virginity of Mary affirm that he never had any marital relations with her, but that is not strictly what is written in the Greek.) In this narrative there is no mention of Mary at all, other than that she was betrothed and pregnant. First-century Nazareth was a male-dominated society, but none the less, if a man had any affection for his betrothed, and was contemplating the extreme step of ending a betrothal, he would surely have discussed the matter with her, and interrogated both her and her family about her unexplained pregnancy. About such matters the Evangelist is silent: he is not interested. His point of concern is not the fact of the Virginal Conception and all that this implies of divine grace and favour. St Matthew is simply interested in showing that while Jesus is the Son of God (because he is 'of the Holy Spirit'), he was at the same time lawfully born in wedlock to a descendant of David, and so he is also a son of David. The story is used to prove something about Jesus. This suggests that the account in St Matthew's gospel is determined by doctrinal considerations; but the fact that St Matthew wrote up the story in this way is not in itself proof that it was not based on fact.

Old Testament Prophecy

The Evangelist uses a verse from the Old Testament to prove the Virginal Conception, prefacing it with his customary phrase: 'All this was done that it might be fulfilled which was spoken of the Lord by the prophet . . .' He then quotes Isaiah 7:14: 'Behold, a virgin shall conceive in her womb and bring forth a son, and they shall call his name Emmanuel, which being interpreted is, God is with us.' In fact the Hebrew text does not contain the Hebrew word for virgin, but a word which means a young woman of marriageable age. However in the Greek text of the Septuagint the word *parthenos* is used. Although its meaning is not confined to those without experience of sexual intercourse, it usually implies this. Assuming that in the Septuagint text the word does here mean a virgin, it is suggested by some that the story of the Virginal Conception grew out of this text. This is most improbable, and finds no support in St Luke's account of the Virginal Conception, where this text is not mentioned. It is far more likely that the story of the Virginal Conception had reached the ears of the Evangelist from an unknown source (probably the Jewish Christian community to which he belonged) and that he (or whoever it was who compiled the series of 'proof texts' in the opening chapters of his gospel) found a text from the Greek version of Isaiah which substantiated the story.

The Matthean Birth Story a Later Addition?

It has been suggested that the birth stories and infancy narratives
in St Matthew's gospel were added later, and that originally the
gospel began at Matthew 3:1: 'In those days came John the Baptist
preaching in the wilderness of Judea, and saying . . .' If this were
the original beginning of St Matthew's gospel it would bring it
into line with the opening of St Mark's gospel. But it would be
a very abrupt opening, with a reference to 'those days' without
any further identification; and John the Baptist would appear as
if from nowhere. The first two chapters of St Matthew's gospel
do not differ in style from that of the rest of the gospel; and they
breathe a Jewish and Palestinian air. There is no reason to assume
that the two gospels necessarily began at the same point. There
is a certain appropriateness about the beginning and end of St
Matthew's gospel as it now stands. It ends with the words: 'Lo,
I am with you alway, even unto the end of the world' and it begins
with the quotation from Isaiah about Immanuel, 'God with us'.
It seems probable therefore that the infancy stories were originally
part of the gospel, and that the argument that they are unhistorical
because they were added later is unsound.

The Source of St Matthew's Account of the Virginal Conception

It is unlikely that the source of Matthew's information about the
Virginal Conception was St Luke's gospel (or even St Luke's
source), since in that gospel the tale is told entirely from the point
of view of Mary, and Joseph appears only as a shadowy figure.
We have no way by which to identify Matthew's source.
However, if it is based on fact, the source must go back to Joseph
himself. Joseph, as we have already noted, probably died before
the public ministry of Jesus began. If Joseph did speak of these
matters, whom would he have told? We have already surmised
that St Matthew's account does not come from a female source.
It is conceivable that he told his other sons born of his earlier
marriage. We have already seen that at the beginning of Jesus'

ministry, they thought that he was out of his mind, although in St John's gospel they are shown in a more favourable light. However, it is not easy to imagine circumstances in which Joseph would have told his other sons about the mystery of Jesus' origins. They did not become Jesus' disciples during his ministry. James the Lord's brother did not become a Christian until Jesus appeared to him at his Resurrection. If Joseph did not tell his sons, whom then did he tell? We do not know how the story of the Virginal Conception reached the Jewish Christian community in which and for which it is generally assumed his gospel was written.

The story of Jesus' Virginal Conception in St Matthew's gospel can hardly be separated from the infancy narratives in that gospel, and it is likely that they were composed by the same hand. They are similar in style, they all contain divinely inspired dreams and they are all buttressed by Old Testament 'proof texts'. It is not possible to determine the extent to which the Evangelist wrote up these accounts and the amount which he owed to his sources at this point.

St Matthew's Infancy Narratives

We cannot here enter into great detail over the story of the Magi who came to offer gifts to the infant Jesus, or over the tale of the Holy Family's flight into Egypt and subsequent return. Much effort has gone into attempting to verify details of the story about the Magi (and in the past I have tried to make my own contribution to this).[7] None of the events which these stories record have been positively disproved. They may be based on actual events. At the same time it can hardly be denied that the stories themselves have been written up more in the style of folk stories than of historical occurrences. The Evangelist is not so much concerned with the events themselves as with their meaning. The story of the Magi describes worship by Gentiles of the infant Jesus; and although the gospel shows signs of being written within a Jewish Christian community, there are many indications that the author believed that the gospel is also for Gentiles. The references to Herod and the slaughter of the innocents at Bethlehem show that forces of evil surrounded Jesus from the day of his birth. The story of the flight from Egypt and subsequent return demonstrates how the history of the Chosen People was recapitulated in the life of the Messiah.

The way in which these stories are told suggests that they may have been intended to be understood within the well established Jewish tradition of *haggadah*, that is to say, stories told for edification without much concern for their historical foundation. If this be the case with the infancy narratives, it could also be the case over the story of Jesus' Virginal Conception. Even so, this does not in itself disprove the Virginal Conception as a historical fact. Even if St Matthew himself wrote up the story of the dream which dissuaded Joseph from divorcing Mary, this does not necessarily mean that the Virginal Conception is unhistorical. The Evangelist seems concerned only with Joseph's reaction to the news that Mary was pregnant and with his obedience to the instructions given him in the dream. Indeed, the Evangelist seems almost to *assume* the truth of the Virginal Conception, which suggests that the tradition about it was well established within his Christian community.

Probable Date of St Matthew's Gospel

We do not know when St Matthew's gospel was written. A few scholars hold that it is the earliest gospel, and that St Mark's gospel is an abbreviation of it. Most scholars believe that underlying our present St Matthew's gospel there is a collection of sayings which goes back to Matthew the Apostle, and which gave the gospel its name. Although I personally think he has made out a powerful case, Bishop John Robinson has not won general support for his contention that the stories and sayings collection about Jesus began to be formed way back in the Thirties and Forties, and that the synoptic gospels, including St Matthew's gospel, began to be formed in the Fifties, and that they were all published before AD 70. The well known commentator, A. H. McNeile, has won more general agreement for his conclusion that the internal evidence of the gospel, together with its relationship to the other gospels 'forbid a date earlier than *c.* AD 80, but do not require one later than AD 100'.[9]

Even if we assume the 'best case', and accept Bishop Robinson's argument that St Matthew's gospel was written in the Sixties, and if we also assume that the Evangelist himself wrote up his infancy narratives, they will still have been written some seventy years after the events which they record, on the supposition that Jesus was born around 7 BC. If Mary was about 14 when she married, and if she lived until she was 50 (which gives her a generous life span for those days), she would have died around AD 43, at least twenty years before St Matthew wrote up the story of the Virginal Conception. (Of course she might have lived on until old age in her seventies, but if that were the case, it is odd that there is no further account of her in reputable Christian historical sources after she is mentioned in the first chapter of the Acts of the Apostles.)

The gospels themselves are a witness to the faithful way in which sayings of Jesus and stories about Jesus could be handed down in oral tradition before they were committed to writing, although some changes certainly took place, and in some cases the alteration between the accounts of the same saying or incident in the different gospels is very marked. There was plenty of time for the story of the Virginal Conception to have developed, as stories did develop about the birth of great men. On the other hand there could have been a genuine tradition about Virginal Conception, at first entrusted to intimates but later surfacing within the Jewish Christian tradition to which St Matthew belonged. Much more evidence remains to be considered before a judgement can be made.

Chapter 4

St Luke's Gospel

The primary evidence for the Virginal Conception is found in St Luke's gospel. It is therefore necessary to examine with special care not only its contents but also its credentials. The author states these at the beginning of his work in a short formal preface, as was quite usual among Greek authors of the time. He writes:

> For as much as many have taken in hand to set forth in order a declaration of those things which are most surely believed among us, even as they delivered them unto us, which from the beginning were eyewitnesses and ministers of the word; it seemed good to me also, having had perfect understanding of all things from the very first, to write unto thee, excellent Theophilos, that thou mightest know the certainty of those things wherein thou hast been instructed.

The preface applies to the gospel as a whole rather than just to the birth and infancy narratives which immediately follow it; but it is important to note exactly what it does and what it does not affirm. The Evangelist claims to have spoken to eyewitnesses of the gospel as well as to the 'ministers of the word' who publicize it. This is hardly surprising if the author is indeed St Luke, the beloved physician who accompanied Paul on part of his journeyings, and who went with him to Jerusalem and was present when the Apostle was arrested and later taken by boat to Rome. He would have had plenty of opportunity, both in Caesarea where he stayed for some time, and also in Jerusalem, to speak to 'eyewitnesses and ministers of the word'.

Secondly, St Luke did not claim to be the first to write about Jesus. He writes that many have done this before him. It is likely that he would have had access to some of these other collections of material. Indeed, he almost certainly used St Mark's gospel in the compilation of his own gospel. Possibly he had also read St Matthew's gospel, but more probably he, like St Matthew, used a sayings collection (usually known as Q from the German *quelle* (source)). It is also possible that some of the material which alone of the four Evangelists he used, came from another written source.

Thirdly, St Luke did not claim to have perfect historical knowledge of everything that was said or done in the life and ministry of Jesus. What he did claim was to have perfect *understanding* of everything from the first. The distinction is important. St Luke insisted that it was his interpretation of the Gospel which was correct.

Finally he stated that his object in writing was to make known the certainty of those things which had formed the object of his reader's Christian instruction. Here again it is important to understand what is meant. It is very unlikely that, at this early stage in the life of the Church, Christian catechesis (that is to say, instruction given to converts) required belief in the Virginal Conception of Christ. But it certainly would have included teaching about Jesus as the Son of God, and of course as the Christ (Jewish Messiah). His birth and infancy narratives would indeed provide for his readers the 'certainty of these things'.

St Luke's preface does not claim historical accuracy in every detail. We know by studying what he wrote that he is not always totally accurate. Occasionally, as we shall see, St Luke made a mistake. Sometimes he deliberately made small changes, or even large alterations in material which he obtained from other sources. We can see this by the way in which he sometimes used St Mark's gospel, and in the changes he probably made to the material which he shared with St Matthew's gospel. We can be fairly certain that such changes were made by St Luke himself because one of the characteristics of his gospel is his concern for theological consistency. Professor Conzelmann has made a careful analysis of these differences, which are often small and subtle, and in this

way he has brought into the open this theological tendency in
his writing.[10] St Luke's great gift of creative writing can be seen
in the companion work to his gospel, the Acts of the Apostles.
Indeed, some have found that they cannot attribute the Acts of
the Apostles to St Luke, because of the difficulty in attributing
to an actual companion of Paul what appear to be grave
discrepancies between the Acts and the evidence of Paul's own
letters. Whatever view is taken about the authorship of Acts (and
I personally find myself able to attribute it to St Luke), it is
impossible to deny that he could sit light to historical accuracy
in matters where he must have known what happened, although
we are entitled to assume that the Evangelist believed that the
changes that he made brought out the inner meaning of the events
and sayings which he recorded, and so they helped his readers
to understand them.

Nowadays we tend to approach these matters in the light of
our modern assumptions about how history should be written,
and from a very different perspective from that of the ancient
world. In ancient Greek writings it was considered quite
appropriate to put a speech into someone's mouth, although in
fact it was the author's free composition. Thucydides often did
this in his *History of the Peloponnesian War*. When we turn from
Greek to Jewish culture, we find a well-established Jewish
tradition of *haggadah*, consisting of a form of rabbinical
interpretation and exposition of Scripture which aimed not at
historical accuracy but at edification, and which might involve
creative writing which sat light to the historical facts.

These considerations do not cast doubt upon the substantial
accuracy of St Luke's gospel; but it is necessary to remind
ourselves that the idea of 'scientific history' – that is to say,
historical facts accurately described without interpretation – is
a modern one (and a false one at that); and we must not try to
impose it on a tradition to which it is alien. A 'high' view of
Scripture must include a proper understanding of the different
forms of biblical writing and the aims and intentions of the various
biblical authors. We must not attribute to them methods and aims
which were not theirs. They deserve better of us than that.

These preliminary thoughts should not incline us to write off St Luke's birth and infancy narratives before they have been considered. At the same time they remind us that the historical accuracy of their contents is not guaranteed by their inclusion within the canon of Scripture. The narratives need to be examined in some detail before a judgement can be made.

The Date of St Luke's Gospel

The majority of scholars think that St Luke's gospel was written after AD 70. They base this mostly on the references to the fall of Jerusalem in that year, and the consequent dispersal of its inhabitants. There are references to this in chapter 21 (and in chapters 19 and 22) which they believe, when compared to parallel passages in St Mark's gospel, support this conclusion. At the same time they would hold that the gospel could not have been written after the New Testament collection of St Paul's epistles was in circulation, because it seems to show some knowledge of their contents. (It is possible that the publication of the Acts of the Apostles stimulated a search for his letters in the ecclesiastical archives of the main cities mentioned in the work, and this led to their collection and publication.) This points to a date after AD 70 but before AD 90, and the period AD 80-5 is thought to be most likely.

However, an earlier date cannot be ruled out. Those passages in St Luke's gospel which predict the coming fall of Jerusalem can be explained as genuine prophecy which makes use of different Old Testament imagery from that used in the other gospels in order to predict the coming doom of the capital city. If this is the case, then the gospel can, despite all the literary, historical and theological difficulties, be attributed to St Luke himself. According to early Christian tradition, found in the Anti-Marcionite prologues (*c.* AD 160-80), Luke was a Syrian of Antioch, a doctor by profession, who became a disciple of the Apostles, and later a follower of St Paul, accompanying him up to the time of his martyrdom. (If this is the case, those passages in the Acts which are written in the first person plural – usually known as the 'We passages' – are probably excerpts from Luke's own travel diary.) According to the Acts, Paul was under house arrest in Rome in AD 60, and we know from other sources that he was martyred, together with Peter, after the fire of Rome in AD 64. It could be that St Luke's gospel and the Acts were completed during this period. It is possible that the Acts were never intended to be more than the story of how the Gospel went from Jerusalem to Rome; but the rather abrupt conclusion with Paul under house arrest, and without any indication of the result of his appeal to Caesar, suggests that the book was completed during this period.

Even if we assume this earlier date, a period of some seventy years would have elapsed between the time when Jesus was conceived and the completion of the Lucan writings, while a later date would produce an ever longer period. This however should not in itself impugn the veracity of St Luke's birth and infancy narratives. If we assume that Mary died in her late fifties, and the material emanated from her in her later years, the gap is narrowed to little more than twenty-five years. While there would have been plenty of time for traditions about Mary to develop within this period, we cannot rule out the possibility – some would say the strong probability – that the Lucan material is based on sound tradition which emanated from the mother of Jesus herself.

The Original Beginning of St Luke's Gospel

Some scholars think that St Luke's gospel originally began at Luke 3:1 with the date which marks the beginning of John the Baptist's ministry. (This date is complex, and it is not easy to reconcile all the references of which it is composed.) It may well be the case that the original draft of St Luke's gospel began at this point: we have no means of knowing for certain. It depends on his method of composition. Some think that he used St Matthew's gospel, because some of his contents are so similar. There is however more general agreement that he did not, but that he did draw on a collections of sayings (Q) which St Matthew also used. It is thought by some that he began his compilation by combining Q with his own special material, and expanded this later when he came across St Mark's gospel; and then finally he added the birth and infancy narratives. He may have been collecting material when he went with Paul up to Jerusalem, first spending some time at Caesarea on the coast, and then going up to the capital.

Luke lodged in Jerusalem, together with Paul, in the house of an old disciple, Mnason of Crete; and he had earlier stayed at Caesarea in the house of Philip the Evangelist, one of the 'Seven'. Philip had four daughters, all of whom 'prophesied'; a charismatic family. These women seem to have been well known in the primitive Church, and just as Luke would have picked up material about Jesus' public ministry from Jerusalem and from Philip the Evangelist, so he may have heard the traditions underlying his birth and infancy narratives from these women. St Luke had a particular concern for women: he mentions more women in his gospel than any of the other Evangelists. He could have heard from these women the tradition about the Virginal Conception, and he may have decided at a later stage when he was in Rome to include this material in the finished version of his gospel. All this, of course, is pure supposition; but he must have taken his material from some source.

One of the difficulties about this theory of 'Proto-Luke' is that it does not easily provide an explanation about the way in which St Luke's original draft of his gospel survived the shipwreck off Malta when Luke was accompanying Paul to Rome. Again, St Mark's gospel is usually associated with Rome, and it would seem likely that Luke first came across it when he was in the capital. This is not easily reconciled with the Proto-Luke hypothesis. But there are many possibilities, and no certainty can be achieved about his method of composition. Even if the birth and infancy narratives were the last ingredients of his gospel, it would be quite wrong to regard them as suspect for this reason. A late source can contain more trustworthy material than an earlier one.

Style and Characteristics of St Luke's Infancy Narratives

The first two chapters of St Luke's gospel, which contain five infancy and birth narratives and one story of Jesus' boyhood, form a continuous whole. All of them, as we have already noted, are told from a woman's point of view (in contrast to St Matthew's gospel, where they are told from a man's point of view). These two chapters are in marked contrast to the rest of St Luke's gospel. They contain phrases reminiscent of the Old Testament (e.g. 'And it came to pass in those days' and 'And, lo, the angel of the Lord came upon them'). They have a strong Palestinian flavour, with their emphasis on the hope of a national Messiah and on the misfortune of childlessness; and they also show some knowledge of procedure at the Jewish Temple in Jerusalem. For this reason it has been suggested that they are based on a Hebrew source, or, more probably, a source in Aramaic, the language spoken in Palestine in New Testament times. (Aramaic bears the same kind of relation to classical Hebrew as contemporary English to Anglo-Saxon.) If this source was already in written form, Luke must have altered it considerably, for the infancy narratives contain clear echoes of the Septuagint (the Greek version of the Bible) and they also bear distinctive marks of Luke's good Greek style. (Luke did not actually write the best Greek in the New Testament: that distinction must be given to the author of the Epistle to the Hebrews.) It seems probable therefore (although there can be no proof) that Luke was the first to put these oral traditions about Jesus' conception and birth into writing. We must assume that he would have been sufficiently conversant with Aramaic (or with Hebrew) to translate his sources into Greek. The somewhat archaic style of these narratives raises the question of what Luke intended by writing them in this manner.

The infancy narratives concern the birth both of Jesus and of his cousin John the Baptist. There is some correspondence between them both. For example, there are some parallels between the annunciation of both the births. In both cases an angel announces it. Zacharias is told: 'Thy wife Elizabeth shall bear thee a son, and thou shalt call his name John' while the annunciation to Mary is strangely similar: 'Behold, thou shalt conceive in thy womb, and bear a son, and thou shalt call his name Jesus.'

It has been suggested that one of the sources of the infancy narratives came from the followers of John the Baptist (cf. Acts 19:1–5). This may well be the case, especially so far as the Benedictus (Luke 1:68–79) is concerned. The Visitation by Mary of Elizabeth, however, belongs (as we shall see) not to the traditions about John but to those about Jesus. If the other stories about John did originate from a different source from those about Jesus, Luke has welded them into one continuous tale.

If Luke was the first to put these infancy narratives into writing, they were probably circulating in oral tradition for some time beforehand. We do not know in what form they would have circulated, nor what these earlier traditions consisted of, nor the extent (if any) to which they developed during this period, nor can we be certain to what extent they were coloured by Luke's own characteristic style when he came to write them. We can only surmise.

Old Testament Imagery in St Luke's Infancy Narratives

We have already noted that Luke was as concerned with meaning and theology as with historical accuracy. His particular interests can be seen very clearly by the way in which he has written up the infancy narratives, and by his use of certain words and phrases. These have been subjected to close analysis by René Laurentin.[11] Although few of us today would recognize the nuances in St Luke's writings, we need to remind ourselves of the incomparably greater knowledge of the Old Testament among the first generation of Christians. It was, after all, their only Bible. Long before the invention of printing, and with few scrolls of the Scriptures available, they would have known lots of their Bible by heart. References which seem to us obscure would have been immediately apparent to those who first read St Luke's gospel.

(1) The Annunciation

When the angel Gabriel appeared to Mary (Luke 1:28–33), he told her to rejoice, that the Lord was with her, and that she must not be afraid, that she would conceive in her womb, and that her Son would be a Saviour who would reign for ever. There is a parallel here with Zephaniah 3:15–17, where the 'daughter of Zion' is told to rejoice, that the God of Israel is with her, that Zion must not be afraid, and that he will bring salvation. St Luke, by the way in which he wrote up the story, used the words and imagery of Zephaniah to show that the messianic promises given to the daughter of Zion are fulfilled in the person of Mary.

There is a further parallel in the story of the Annunciation between Luke 1:32f. and 2 Samuel 7:12–16. The angel tells Mary that her son will be great, that he will be called the Son of the Most High, that God will give him the throne of his father David, that he will reign for ever, and of his kingdom there shall be no end. In 2 Samuel, God speaks through the prophet Nathan to David, telling him that he will establish his seed after him, that God will be his father, and he will be his son, that his kingdom will last for ever, and that his throne will be established for ever. The parallelism here is very marked. St Luke is telling the story in such a way that the messianic promises given to David are seen to be fulfilled in the coming of Jesus.

There are yet more overtones to the story. There is some similarity between the tale of the Annunciation, and some passages of the prophet Isaiah. According to Isaiah 7:14 a virgin shall conceive, reminiscent of the phrase 'Thou shalt conceive in thy womb'. The angel came to a village in Galilee, reminiscent of 'Galilee of the nations' (Isaiah 8:23). Mary is told: 'The Holy Spirit shall come upon thee', whereas it is prophesied in Isaiah 11:1f.: 'There shall come forth a rod out of the stem of Jesse, and a branch shall grow out of his roots, and the spirit of the Lord shall rest upon him.' St Luke makes it clear by the words and imagery that he uses that Jesus is the fulfilment of the messianic promises made by the prophet Isaiah.

Even this does not exhaust the Old Testament overtones. The angel tells Mary: 'The power of the Most High shall overshadow thee; therefore that holy thing which shall be born of thee shall be called the Son of God.' This makes use of imagery taken from Exodus 40:35, which describes how Moses was not able to enter into the Ark of the Covenant, because the cloud covered the Tent with its shade, and the glory of the Lord filled the tabernacle. Just as the presence of God himself filled the Tent in the wilderness, so his very presence, Mary was told, would also overshadow her.

This simple passage of nine verses is packed with Old Testament words and imagery. The story of the Annunciation concludes with a reference to the unexpected pregnancy of her cousin Elizabeth, now in her sixth month. This passage seems to be added at this point so as to form a bridge to the story of the Visitation which follows. It is in the sixth month that a baby stirs in its mother's womb.

We have to ask ourselves how this imagery is to be explained. Perhaps the account gives us the actual form of angelic words as they were heard by Mary, and faithfully handed down from her in oral and written tradition. But the correspondences between St Luke and the prophetic passages are to be seen not only in what is said, but also in the way in which the story is told. Could it be that St Luke's mind and imagination are so steeped in Old Testament imagery that he unconsciously used this language and imagery? A third explanation seems equally possible. For all their simplicity and beauty, these passages could have been deliberately written up by St Luke in order to show the fulfilment of Old Testament prophecy in the coming of Jesus. The tales would be *haggadah*, a form of creative writing whose purpose is to achieve a homiletic aim. In this case the intention was to show that Mary recapitulated in her person the Messianic promises given to the 'daughter of Zion' in the Old Testament, that Jesus was indeed the Messiah promised to David who would reign for ever, and that he was not merely the promised Messiah but God himself in the midst of his people.

If this is the case, it should be noted that the two phrases used by St Luke to describe the Virginal Conception ('the power of the Most High shall overshadow thee' and 'the Holy Spirit shall come upon thee') are not descriptions of a Virginal Conception as such but rather imagery taken from the Old Testament to describe the coming of God and his Messiah into his world.

(2) The Visitation

St Luke links the Annunciation to the Visitation, as we have already noted, by means of the angelic announcement to Mary that her cousin Elizabeth, thought to be barren, was in the sixth month of her pregnancy. Mary hurried to the hill country where Elizabeth was staying (traditionally El Karem), so as to share the incredible news of her own pregnancy with someone whom she could trust and who would be likely to be sympathetic. There are some remarkable parallels in St Luke's account to the story in Samuel about the Ark of the Covenant when it was being brought by David to Jerusalem. The incident is found in 2 Samuel 6, when the Ark was in the very neighbourhood where Elizabeth was later to stay. It was brought into the house of Obededom (2 Samuel 6:11), as Mary was later to enter into the house of Zacharias (Luke 1:40). David, who had been frightened by the incident in which Uzziah had lost his life, exclaimed: 'How shall the ark of the Lord come to me?' (2 Samuel 6:9), words which find an unmistakable echo in Elizabeth's exclamation 'Whence is this to me, that the mother of my Lord should come to me?' (Luke 1:43). The ark stayed in the house of Obededom for three months, and similarly Mary stayed with Elizabeth for three months before departing for home (Luke 1:56). Clearly St Luke has deliberately told this story in such a way that Mary corresponds to the ark of God in which the presence of God rested. In other words, Mary is carrying in her womb the very presence of God himself.

A further overtone is to be found in a story concerning Judith, one of the great heroines of Israel. According to the folk tale, she killed Holofernes, the oppressor of the Jews, and when she returned to her own people after perpetrating his death, Ozias exclaimed: 'Blessed art thou of the most high God above all the women of the earth; and blessed be the Lord God . . .' (Judith 13:18). There is a striking correspondence here with the words which Elizabeth exclaims to Mary when her baby stirred within her: 'Blessed art thou among women and blessed is the fruit of thy womb' (Luke 1:42). But there is a subtle and significant difference. Instead of the phrase in Judith 'Blessed is the Lord God' St Luke has 'Blessed is the fruit of thy womb.' St Luke is telling us that the fruit of Mary's womb is indeed the Lord God himself. Once again, we see that Mary is carrying in her womb the very essence of God himself.

Mary responds to Elizabeth with the words of the Magnificat. There is some manuscript evidence (but not much) to ascribe it to Elizabeth instead of Mary. This might suggest that it is not Luke's own original composition, but it might have been a kind of hymn used by the followers of John the Baptist, and later ascribed to Mary (possibly by Luke himself). But this is unlikely because its contents are better suited to Mary. There are many Old Testament echoes in the hymn, pointing towards Israel. (J. M. Creed, in his commentary on St Luke, counts up to twenty!) Most of these are not directly messianic, but if Mary is understood as the 'daughter of Zion', its attribution to her is most appropriate, and indeed all generations *have* called her blessed. The final words of the hymn 'As he promised to our forefathers, Abraham and his seed for ever' is particularly appropriate, because Mary's coming motherhood did indeed mark the fulfilment of the divine promises which began with Abraham. The reference to Abraham, in whom it is promised all the nations of the earth will be blessed, is particularly appropriate in St Luke's gospel, with its universalist tendency. Perhaps the most striking and unexpected phrase in the hymn is the exaltation by God of the humble and meek. God did indeed honour an unknown girl to be the instrument of the Incarnation, and by so doing he has 'shown strength with his arm' by this unique act of divine power.

The story of the Annunciation has been deliberately written so as to use Old Testament imagery to demonstrate the divine nature of the baby growing in the womb of Mary. The story does not in itself prove or disprove the Virginal Conception. It does make clear that the presence of God indwelt the unborn baby. This should not be understood in such a way as to contradict the story of the Spirit descending on Jesus at his baptism, when the divine voice pronounced: 'This is my beloved Son' (Matthew 3:17). This marks the moment not when Jesus became Son of God but when the secret of Jesus' nature was disclosed. In some Old Latin manuscripts of the baptism are added here the words 'This day have I begotten thee'; but this does not deny the Virginal Conception, it merely continues the quotation from Psalm 2:7 so as to mark this moment as the induction of Jesus into the role of the Messiah.

The Visitation narrative faces us with the same question as that of the Annunciation. Do these accounts set out accurately to describe historic events, or do they constitute *haggadah*, beautifully written tales told in order to show, in terms of Old Testament prophecy, the divine nature of the growing babe? The question is important, because if all the infancy and birth narratives hang together, if one is intended to be *haggadah* and not history, this would probably apply to all of them.

(3) The Lucan Account of the Nativity
As in the other stories, so in St Luke's account of the birth of Jesus we find correspondences with the prophetic writings, in particular Micah 5:1–5. In Micah we read: 'And thou, Bethlehem Ephratah, though thou be little among the thousands of Judah, yet out of thee shall come forth unto me that is to be the ruler of Israel, whose goings forth have been from of old, from everlasting.' The passage in Micah continues somewhat obscurely, referring to 'the time that she which travaileth hath brought forth', bringing to mind St Luke's reference to 'the days accomplished that she should be delivered' (Luke 2:6). The next verse is also obscure. In the New English Bible it is translated: 'He shall appear and be their shepherd in the strength of the Lord, in the majesty of the name of the Lord his God, and he shall be a man of peace.' In St Luke's gospel we find also a reference to shepherds in verse 8, to the glory of the Lord in verse 9, and to peace on earth in verse 14.

This reference to Bethlehem in the prophet Micah seems to have been connected by the rabbis with 'the tower of the flock' in Genesis 35:21. The Scriptures were read out in Hebrew in Jesus' day (as of course they still are in synagogues today); but because in those days many could not understand classical Hebrew, there were translations into Aramaic, and these translations were often paraphrases. They are called *targums*, and in the *targum* on Genesis 35:21 we read: 'And Jacob proceeded and spread his tent beyond the tower of the flocks, the place from whence it is to be that the king Messiah will be revealed at the end of the days.'

These are the only references to Bethlehem as the place of birth for the Messiah. If Luke's account of the Nativity is *haggadah*, creative writing which shows the fulfilment of Old Testament prophecy in the actual coming of the Messiah, this passage in Micah, together with the *targum* on Genesis, seems a somewhat tenuous base from which to construct so much – Jesus' birth in a cave in Bethlehem because there was no room at the inn, and the subsequent account of shepherds, after seeing a vision by night, coming and worshipping the new-born baby. (It is just possible that there is a reference to the latter in Hebrews 1:6, which I have argued is an early Epistle:[12] 'And again, when he bringeth the first begotten into the world, he saith, And let all the angels of God worship him.') Did St Luke create these stories out of the Old Testament prophecies, or did he have other sources?

Scholars have ransacked literature to try to find other sources, both for the Nativity and for the Virginal Conception, but their labour has been in vain. There are no parallels in Jewish or pagan literature. The Old Testament describes unexpected births but never 'virgin births'. The nearest Jewish parallel is in the writings of Philo, who wrote in Alexandria during the New Testament period. In his work on the Cherubim we find:

God then sows indeed the seed, but on the other hand bestows as a gift his own offspring which he has sown; for God begets nothing for himself, for God has need of nothing; but he begets all things for those who need to receive them. I will adduce as a sufficient surety of all the things I am saying the most holy

Moses; for he introduces Sarah as being with child not to him who made the visitation, but to him who desired to attain wisdom – and this latter is called Abraham. And in the case of Leah he teaches that more plainly, saying that God opened her womb – and to open the womb is a function of the husband . . . Again, when the all-wise Isaac entreated God, Rebecca, who is perseverance, became pregnant from him who was entreated . . .

This is a striking passage, but those whom Philo mentions are credited with a divine conception, not a *virginal* conception. In any case Philo was interested more in the allegorical meaning of what he wrote than in the events themselves, and so his apparently historical statements need to be treated with caution.

As for pagan literature, parallels have been alleged, among others, in the birth of Osiris, Mithras, Cyrus, Romulus and Remus. None of these provides any real parallel to a virginal conception. The closest perhaps is the conception of Perseus as a result of Zeus coming down on Danaë in a shower of golden rain! It is hard to think of a tale more unlike the Lucan stories, which breathe a Palestinian air very different from those coming out of a Greek or Egyptian milieu. In any case these pagan stories tell a tale of divine lust and not divine love.

Since there are no parallels to Jesus' conception and birth in Jewish or non-Jewish literature, and Micah's prophecies seem to provide such a tenuous base for Luke's creative writing, the presumption would seem to be that they are accounts of what actually happened which did indeed fulfil Micah's prophetic hints of what was to come. However, this involves overcoming a grave historical difficulty.

The Decree of Universal Taxation

The occasion of Joseph and Mary's journey to Bethlehem, according to St Luke, was an imperial decree. 'And it came to pass in those days that there went out a decree from Caesar Augustus that the whole world should be taxed. (And this taxing was first made when Quirinius was governor of Syria.) And all went to be taxed, everyone to his own city' (Luke 2:1–3). St Luke is here telling us that there was a universal registration throughout the whole Roman Empire around the date 7 BC when Jesus was born.

But was there? No such registration under the Emperor Augustus is known. It is scarcely credible that Josephus, who wrote a history of the Jewish people and who was a protégé of the Romans, and who was also very well informed, should not have mentioned such a census (whether universal or local) which took place in 7 BC, or that we should not have heard about the census from Roman sources. But we do know about a census thirteen or fourteen years later, in AD 7. After Archelaus had been deposed by the Romans as King of Judaea, and the province came under direct Roman rule, a census became possible. It would have been out of the question for the Roman government to have conducted a census in Judaea while Herod or Archelaus was ruling as a puppet king set up by the Romans and allied to them. But as soon as Archelaus was deposed, the political situation entirely changed, and such a census became possible. What is more, this later census was actually conducted by Quirinius when he was governor of Syria. Josephus tells us why he mentions that this later census took place in AD 7; it was an innovation and it sparked off a Zealot revolt under Judas of Galilee. But that was many years after the birth of Jesus. Some scholars have tried to salvage St Luke's date by suggesting that Quirinius had an earlier spell as Governor of Syria (for which there is no evidence) and that Luke was only alluding to preparations for this later census which took some time to make; but in reality no such preparations were possible until the province reverted to direct rule.

So Luke seems to have made a mistake. He made other mistakes. For example, he records in Acts a speech by Gamaliel referring to a rebellion by a certain Theudas which, he assumes, had already taken place; but in fact this rebellion took place after the time at which Gamaliel is reported to have made the speech!

If there was no census around 7 BC, there would have been no registration; and if no registration, Joseph and Mary would not have made the journey to Bethlehem, and Jesus would not have been born there. Even if Joseph did own property there (and there is no evidence that he did) he would surely not on this account have made the long journey there with his wife when she was in the last month of her pregnancy. Even if for some reason he did go there with her, there would not have been the great crowd of people in the city who had come there for the registration, and so the inn would not have been full up. There is a further problem. There is no other known instance of a Roman census which involved people going back to their original place of abode. How could the Roman authorities have known that people actually had registered in a distant town if they had to return to their original place of abode? The administrative arrangements for a census which involved people moving around the countryside would have been formidable. Registration for the 'poll tax' in Britain in the twentieth century has been difficult enough, even with the aid of computers, and that at people's actual place of residence. The social upheaval would have been considerable. Although the numbers involved are much larger, a modern parallel to people from near Jerusalem registering in Galilee would be Welsh people living near London returning to Wales in order to register for taxation.

Yet it was registration for Roman taxation which, according to St Luke, was the occasion which gave rise to the birth of Jesus in the city of Bethlehem in accordance with Micah's prophesy. Remove the census, and the story collapses. Could there have been an otherwise unknown local registration at the time of Jesus' birth which required people to return to their original place of abode? Although for the reasons given above it is exceedingly improbable, it cannot be called inconceivable. But the most probable explanation is that Luke had heard of the census in AD 7, and he brought it forward to coincide with the birth of Jesus which took place around 7 BC, either not knowing or ignoring the fact that such a census would not have been possible until Judaea was under direct Roman rule. After all Luke was writing half a century later. Possibly this mistake had occurred earlier in the source from which Luke took his account of Christ's Nativity.

On the other hand the Old Testament overtones in the account of the Nativity are similar to those found in the other infancy narratives of St Luke's gospel, making it probable that it was the Evangelist himself who first wrote them all up.

These difficulties over the date of the census suggest that the story of Jesus' birth in St Luke's gospel may have been *haggadah*, exquisitely written 'idylls of the king' which describe the birth of the Messiah, showing that God has indeed visited his people in accordance with prophecy, and that he has put down the mighty from their seat and exalted the humble and meek. The tale of Jesus' nativity in Bethlehem is rightly loved and valued, because it gives concrete expression to our deepest convictions about God's love and compassion in being born as a defenceless babe, about his solidarity with the homeless in himself being born far from home, and about his welcome by those whom the world despises, for the first greeting he received was from shepherds. (In those days shepherds did not meet with the sentimental approval of well-wishers: they were regarded as ruffianly types, and that is why in the fourth gospel Jesus describes himself not as the shepherd but as 'the good shepherd'.) Dearly as we love these stories, we have to face the historical facts. Of course if we do hold these accounts of Jesus to be *haggadah*, this does not disprove the historicity of the Virginal Conception. But the stories in the first two chapters of St Luke's gospel form a continuous whole, and to cast doubts on the historicity of the main story in the series inevitably casts its shadow over the other stories in these two chapters.

An Interpolation into the Story of the Annunciation

The stories in these first two chapters have been considered in this study as a continuous whole. Some scholars however have suggested that an addition has been made to the account of the Annunciation by inserting the announcement of the Virginal Conception, which was not in the original version of the story. Since there is no textual evidence for the interpolation, these critics agree that it must have been made by the Evangelist himself. This in itself would not disprove the historicity of the Virginal Conception, because reliable information might conceivably have come into the possession of St Luke later, after he had written his first draft of the story; but if this theory is correct, it would at least cast doubt on its historical veracity.

Those who hold this theory believe that Luke 1:34 and 35 were added later: 'Then Mary said unto the angel, How can this be, seeing I know not a man? And the angel answered and said unto her, The Holy Ghost shall come upon thee, and the power of the Highest shall overshadow thee: therefore that holy thing which shall be born of thee shall be called the Son of God.'

These verses however are not the only occasions when a Virginal Conception is implied by St Luke. In Luke 1:27 Mary is twice described as a virgin, a somewhat unnecessary emphasis in an age when every girl was assumed to be virginal before her wedding. Again, in Luke 2:5 Mary is said to be 'betrothed to him (Joseph), being great with child'. This verse seems to have caused some embarrassment to the copyists, for there are several variant readings at this point. It must imply the Virginal Conception as without this the verse can only mean that Jesus was the natural son of Mary and Joseph, conceived during their betrothal but before their wedding. If the Evangelist inserted Luke 1:34f., he must have made also these consequential alterations, as well as inserting 'as was supposed' in his genealogy, without which Jesus would be described simply as the son of Joseph.

The language of the two verses in Luke 1:34f., which it is alleged have been inserted into the original version, is both Jewish and Lucan. On what grounds can such an interpolation be substantiated? Various reasons have been given. First, it has been rightly said that the main emphasis in the Lucan birth stories is on the coming of Jesus the Messiah. But this would not rule out the inclusion of the Virginal Conception, since Jesus has already been shown to be Joseph's legal son and heir. Secondly, it is said that the reference in Luke 2:41 to Mary and Joseph as the 'parents of Jesus' and in Luke 2:48 to Joseph as his 'father' show that the account of the Virginal Conception must be a later addition. But this is how they were commonly known. How else was the Evangelist to describe them? Thirdly, it is said that the question 'How can this be, seeing that I know not a man?' is a quite inappropriate response by a young girl betrothed to be married when she is told that she is going to have a baby, since the angel did not tell her that the conception would take place before her marriage. She would have hoped and expected to bear a child. John the Baptist was struck dumb for disbelieving that Elizabeth would become pregnant, even though she was past the normal age of childbearing. (Roman Catholics understand the phrase 'seeing that I know not a man' to imply a vocation to perpetual celibacy, but that is reading into the text more than is actually there.) However, if Mary understood the angel's words to mean that she would *immediately* become pregnant – and Luke obviously intends this by the way he recounts the story – her response seems entirely appropriate.

These arguments in favour of an interpolation can easily be answered. But there is a still more decisive consideration. The whole structure of the chapter is built around miraculous births; first to Zacharias and Elizabeth in their old age, and then to Mary through her Virginal Conception. The similarity between the two is marked, and what is said to one applies equally to the other: 'With God nothing shall be impossible' (Luke 1:37). Remove Luke 1:34f. and there is literary bathos; first, a wondrous conception on the part of Elizabeth, and then an ordinary conception on the part of Mary. St Luke, with his great gifts of creative writing, could not possibly have written a chapter with such an anticlimax. Despite the arguments of well known biblical scholars such as Harnack[13] and Vincent Taylor[14], there is no valid case to be made for a later interpolation by St Luke of these two verses into his original version of the Annunciation. (One cannot help wondering whether 'the wish being father to the thought' underlies such a theory.) The Evangelist must have regarded the two verses as an essential part of his story.

The Other Infancy Stories in St Luke's Gospel

The accounts of the annunciation to Zacharias of his wife Elizabeth's coming pregnancy and the subsequent naming of the child after he was born concern John the Baptist. They are likely to have been current among his followers. There are Old Testament overtones to be found in these passages, especially the birth of a child to Abraham and Sarah in their old age, and also the appearance of an angel who announced to Manoah the gift to his barren wife of a child who was to be a Nazirite from birth, like John the Baptist drinking no strong drink. The information about temple procedures in St Luke's stories is accurate, except for the minor point that Zacharias is said to have been alone at the altar of incense when he received his vision, while temple regulations required four other priests to be present there with him.

The stories about the Circumcision of Jesus and his Presentation in the Temple read like straightforward historical accounts, except perhaps for the prophecies of Simeon and Anna. In his account of the Purification, the Evangelist writes of 'their cleansing', whereas Leviticus requires only the cleansing of the woman; but the point should not be pressed. If the Virginal Conception is historical, it is perhaps odd that Mary should have been so surprised at Simeon's prophecy (Luke 2:33), but once again this point can hardly be pressed. The phrases of the Nunc Dimittis 'for mine eyes have seen thy salvation' and 'a light to lighten the Gentiles' recall Messianic prophesies in Isaiah 52:10 and 42:6. We cannot tell whether this canticle pre-dates Luke, just as we do not know whether there was a source for the prophetic words attributed to Simeon and Anna. To decide this, it is necessary to consider the nature of the first two chapters as a whole.

The last story in the series is not strictly a story of Jesus' infancy but of his childhood. His family was returning from Jerusalem to Nazareth after the Passover. Jesus was not to be found in the company; but later he was discovered in the Temple, discussing religious matters with the authorities there. The point of the story is to show Jesus' consciousness of his true nature as Son of God.

His mother is reported to have said to him: 'Son, why hast thou dealt thus with us? Behold, thy father and I have sought thee sorrowing' to which Jesus is said to have replied: 'How is it that ye sought me? Wist ye not that I must be about my Father's business' (Luke 2:49). It is not so very surprising that Jesus was found in the Temple at that age: Josephus tells us a somewhat similar story about himself. But it is perhaps surprising that Jesus should have rather self-consciously repudiated Joseph as his father (for doubtless he had been brought up to regard him as such) and to speak of God as his Father in his place.

Presumably Luke obtained this story from the same source as others in the series. It is not impossible that the tale accurately depicts what happened. It seems just as likely (or perhaps more likely) that, however the story may have originated, it was developed after the Resurrection, when the divine nature of Jesus had been recognized by the early Church (but this is not to say that the story lacks all historical foundation: Jesus probably did stay behind in the Temple). For doctrinal reasons it may have become phrased in such a way that a contrast between the two fathers was emphasized. If this is the case, it is easier to reconcile it with what happened at Jesus' baptism, when we are told Jesus first became conscious of his divine sonship (mediated to him through the words of the Psalm 'Thou art my son'). This overwhelming experience, rather like a conversion, made such an impact upon him that he immediately gave up his secular vocation and began his public ministry.

The Lucan Genealogy

What evidence about the Virginal Conception can be gleaned from St Luke's version of Jesus' genealogy? He placed it after his account of Jesus' baptism, in contrast to St Matthew who placed his at the beginning of his gospel. This lends some weight to the idea that originally St Luke's gospel began at the present chapter 3 (the 'Proto-Luke hypothesis'), because then the genealogy would have been at the beginning of the initial draft of the gospel instead of in its present rather strange position.

There are several differences between St Matthew's and St Luke's versions. In the first place, St Luke starts from Adam instead of Abraham, in keeping with his universalist tendencies; and the pedigree runs backwards from Jesus rather than forwards towards him as in Matthew. Secondly, it diverges from St Matthew's version in two places. Instead of going from David to Solomon, the line is traced through Nathan, another son of David. The two genealogies converge at Zerubbabel and his father, and then they diverge again and do not join up again until Joseph himself is reached. Many attempted explanations have been given for these differences, such as descent through a levirate line, or descent through the line of priesthood rather than the line of royalty, or even by supposing that St Luke traces Mary's ancestry. A further difference is to be found in St Luke's inclusion of a name which is only found in the Septuagint, and not in the original Hebrew version of the Bible.

The importance of St Luke's genealogy lies in that it shows that Jesus was descended from David. The genealogy must either have been compiled by the Evangelist himself, or, if he got it from a source, that source could not have been aware of the Virginal Conception. While St Luke might have written (or added) 'as was supposed' when writing of Joseph as the father of Jesus, this could hardly have been written by anyone else who had composed the genealogy to stand on its own. Even if Luke did get the genealogy from some source which knew nothing of the Virginal Conception, this cannot be said to disprove its historicity in the case of St Luke's gospel any more than it can in the case of St Matthew's gospel.

Comparison of the Birth Stories in St Matthew's and St Luke's Gospels

Is it possible to combine the infancy narratives in both gospels? The answer to this question is highly relevant to the question of their historicity. Presumably Mary had been pregnant for more than a month before she was aware of the fact. So it must have been more than a month after her conception that Joseph married her (Matthew). The impression is given by Matthew that Joseph married her as soon as he found out about her pregnancy. On the other hand we are told by St Luke that as soon as she knew she was to be pregnant she went with haste to the hill country to see her cousin, and stayed there for three months. Joseph would hardly have married her in a hurry and then let her make off in haste for a lengthy visit to her cousin: after all, the essence of marriage in those days was taking the bride to the husband's house. So if she went straightway to see Elizabeth, she could not have been married until she returned, well into the fourth month of her pregnancy, only five months at most before the birth of her baby. She would by then have been beginning to look pregnant at the time of her marriage; and in any case the birth would have seemed impossibly premature to have been conceived since the wedding, and this would certainly have given rise to gossip on the part of those who knew when the wedding had taken place. Of course if the baby was born away from home in Bethlehem (Luke), the townsfolk in Nazareth might not have known exactly when the birth took place, although these matters usually get about. It seems that the couple must have remained in the area of Bethlehem for some time (did they move out of the cave where the birth took place?), if they went (presumably from Bethlehem) to the Temple nearby in Jerusalem for Mary's purification a month after the birth – forty days, to be precise. The visit of the Magi, if it was a historical event, would have taken place after this (Matthew), because it was on the departure of the Magi that Joseph was warned in a dream to leave at once for Egypt, which he did forthwith (Matthew).

On this reckoning there is no formal inconsistency between the two accounts. On the other hand it is only in St Luke's gospel that Nazareth appears as the family home. In St Matthew's gospel Nazareth is not mentioned until the return from Egypt when the family settled there, having been warned not to return to Bethlehem. The birth and infancy narratives in the two gospels are entirely different, and all they have in common is the Virginal Conception of Jesus and his birth in Bethlehem in fulfilment of Old Testament prophecy.

Four possible relationships between the two sets of stories are possible.

1. The two accounts are both historically accurate, and despite the difficulties which have been discussed in this chapter, they may be reconciled in the way attempted above.

2. One of the accounts only is historically accurate, and the other consists of *haggadah*, that is to say, creative tales illustrative of spiritual truths about Jesus' origins. (The Matthean stories would seem to fit this category better, because of the particular difficulties discussed in the previous chapter.)

3. Both sets of birth and infancy narratives are *haggadah* and none of the details of these tales is historically accurate, except for the fact of the Virginal Conception.

4. The stories in both gospels are *haggadah*, and while they may contain traditions based on historical reminiscence, none of them (including the Virginal Conception) describe actual historical events, although they contain important theological and spiritual truths in language of great beauty.

We are not yet in a position to make up our minds about the most likely of these four possibilities until the rest of the evidence about the Virginal Conception has been examined.

Chapter 5

The Rest of the New Testament

The three synoptic gospels are not the earliest books of the New Testament. The Epistles of St Paul, for example, are earlier. The rest of the New Testament, as well as the books already considered, needs to be considered in relation to the Virginal Conception of Jesus. If we can find evidence there for belief that Jesus was conceived without a human father, this would tend to confirm the evidence of the synoptic gospels of St Matthew and St Luke. The absence of any reference to this belief, if that is found to be the case, would need to be evaluated. It might be because there was no Virginal Conception. On the other hand it might be that the other writers had no particular need to refer to it, or that the Virginal Conception, although a fact of history, was unknown to them. First, however, there is another gospel to consider.

St John's Gospel

There is disagreement whether or not the author of the fourth gospel knew about the Virginal Conception of Jesus. In part the answer may lie in whether he knew St Matthew's and St Luke's gospels. It is never easy to determine quite what lies beneath the surface of this gospel. One can strip off layers of meaning, like peeling skins from an onion. There is often, too, a subtle irony in what is written.

There is no account of the birth of Jesus in St John's gospel. After the preface, the opening leads straight into the ministry of John the Baptist and Jesus' baptism at his hands. In the preface itself, which comprises the first eighteen verses of the book, we find immediately after a reference to the Word made flesh: 'But as many as received him, to them gave he power to become the sons of God, even to those which believe in his name; which were born not of blood, nor of the will of the flesh, nor of the will of man, but of God' (John 1:12f.). The Evangelist here is referring not to birth, but to rebirth. He is saying that this kind of rebirth is not physical, nor does it spring from natural impulses, nor can it be brought about by an act of the human will: it is the gift of God. Since however this passage comes immediately after his reference to the Incarnation, it could be that he had in mind here a parallelism between birth and rebirth, that is, the Virginal Conception and spiritual regeneration. In both cases the initiative comes not from man but from God. Does this parallelism lie under the surface of the text? We cannot be certain. Even if there is a reference here to the Virginal Conception, it hardly sheds light on its historicity.

In chapter 7 the 'brethren of the Lord' are mentioned, trying to persuade Jesus to go up to Jerusalem for the Feast of Tabernacles, so that his disciples could see his works. If this account is historical, Jesus' brothers no longer believed (as they did near the beginning of his ministry, according to St Mark's gospel) that Jesus was out of his mind. On the contrary, they appear rather to be on his side.

Jesus, having refused his brothers' advice, is said to have gone up to Jerusalem later on his own, and openly to have taught in the Temple. In the course of a dispute between Jesus and the Jews in the Temple courts, some of the Jews are reported to have said: 'Do the rulers know that this is the very Christ? Howbeit we know this man whence he is; but when Christ cometh no man knoweth whence he is' (John 7:26f.). Jesus is reported as crying out in response: 'You both know me and you know whence I am; and I am not come of myself, but he who sent me is true, whom ye know not' (John 7:28). Jesus, by his reply, clearly implies that he comes from God, but this tells us nothing about the circumstances of his conception. What did the Jews mean by saying that they knew where Jesus came from, but they did not know the Messiah's origins? We cannot be certain. There was, as we have seen, a tradition that the Messiah would be born in Bethlehem, but these Jews may not have realized this. As for where Jesus came from, it is likely that they were referring to Nazareth, where he had lived before beginning his public ministry.

It is rather perplexing, in the light of this exchange, to read in the same chapter (although on a different occasion), exactly the opposite, when the Evangelist records a difference of opinion about whether Jesus is the Christ. 'Others said, This is the Christ. But some said, Shall Christ come out of Galilee? Hath not the Scripture said, that Christ cometh of the seed of David, and out of the town of Bethlehem, where David was?' (John 7:41f.: the scriptural reference here of course is to Micah 5.) Maybe the Evangelist was simply describing different views held by different sets of people. But there could well be a deeper layer of meaning. The Evangelist may have known the tradition that Jesus, despite his home in Galilee, was in fact born in Bethlehem. There may be a certain irony underlying his description of this conversation. If this were so, there might be here some independent confirmation of the Virginal Conception. On the other hand, he might merely have gleaned this from his knowledge of the synoptic gospels.

In the next chapter, the author records further controversy between Jesus and the Jews in the Temple courts. The altercation becomes very sharp on both sides. The argument turns on who are the true children of Abraham. We know from the writings of St Paul that descent from Abraham was a matter of controversy between Jews and Christians (Romans 5:9ff. and Galatians 3:14–19). The synoptic gospels tell us that John the Baptist caused offence in his preaching to the Jews on this theme (Matthew 3:9; Luke 3:8). According to St John's gospel, Jesus told the Jews that they were not Abraham's children because by their lives they denied him. Later in the chapter Jesus accused them of being children of their father the devil. The Jews replied to this with the words: 'We be not born of fornication: we have one Father, even God' (John 8:41).

This may well be merely a case of returning insult for insult. On the other hand there may well be again a certain irony if the Fourth Evangelist knew of the Virginal Conception. He may have known the Jewish libel that Jesus was the illegitimate son of a Roman soldier, Panthera (although this is usually regarded as a later Jewish response to the Christian claim of the Virginal Conception). If this is the case, there may be a further irony intended by the self-righteous way in which the Jews continued: 'We have one Father, even God', if the Evangelist believed that in fact it was Jesus and not the Jews who had 'one father, even God'. However such irony may not have been intended, because in the next verse Jesus says: 'I proceeded forth and come from God' which refers to his eternal origin rather than to the mode of his conception. Even if an indirect reference to the Virginal Conception was intended, it hardly sheds light on its historicity. We may summarize this enquiry by saying that it is possible that the fourth gospel does make some indirect references to the Virginal Conception, but that, if so, these do not lie on the surface of his narrative, and so they cannot be regarded as primary evidence for its truth.

St Paul

Paul wrote his letters earlier than the four Evangelists wrote their gospels, so that any reference to the Virginal Conception from him would have special value. Some people think that there is special significance in what he wrote to the Galatians:

> When the fulness of the time was come, God sent forth his Son, made of a woman, made under the law, to redeem them that were under the law, that we might receive the adoption of sons. And because ye are sons, God hath sent forth the Spirit of his Son into your hearts, crying, Abba, Father.
>
> (Galatians 4:4–6)

Paul's phrase 'made of a woman' has seemed odd to some. 'Made of a man' would seem more appropriate as the Jewish idea of conception was that a woman was simply the vessel in which the seed of man was nurtured until the time of birth. So it is sometimes said that Paul here was referring to Jesus' Virginal Conception, because he did not mention his human father, but simply wrote that God sent forth his pre-existent Son who 'came into being' (*genomenon*) out of a woman; i.e. Mary provided his humanity and only God and Mary were involved in his conception. Most commentators, however, regard this as reading the Virginal Conception into the text rather than out of it. It was the act of Incarnation that Paul was emphasizing. The phrase 'made of a woman' means no more than that Jesus was fully human as well as fully divine. There is no suggestion in the passage as a whole that Paul was referring here to the mode of Jesus' conception as a human being.

It has also been suggested that the phrase 'adoption of sons' implies a reference to the Virginal Conception. Jesus was adopted as the son of Joseph, who by his marriage to Mary became legally his father. We in our turn are not children of God by right, but we have been adopted as his sons through our identification with Christ. It is perfectly true that the idea of adoption is a particularly happy one if St Paul did have here in mind the Virginal Conception; but the text itself points in a different direction. The phrase 'Abba, Father' refers to the baptism of Jesus, when he heard the divine voice 'Thou art my Son'. Abba is the Aramaic word for father (or rather, 'daddy') which would not have been known to the Greek-speaking Christians in Galatia. It was retained in the early Church with reference to baptism because it was treasured as the actual word which Jesus had used for God. So the idea behind Paul's thinking here is that Christians have shared in the baptism of Christ, the 'one baptism' of Ephesians 4:5. What was his by right is ours by adoption. It is baptism rather than conception that Paul had in mind when he wrote of Christians' adoption to sonship.

Paul at the beginning of his Epistle to the Romans gives what reads like a formal, almost credal, statement about 'his Son Jesus

Christ, which was made of the seed of David according to the flesh' (Romans 1:3). He could hardly have made use of such a formula if he knew about the Virginal Conception. It is one thing to be legally adopted into the house of David, but quite another to be born of the seed of David. If the Virginal Conception was known to those whom he met, he would have found out about it on his visits to Jerusalem, especially during the private visit which he made when he first visited the capital for a fortnight to see Peter. If he had known of it later, he did not think that it was sufficiently important to be mentioned in any of his later correspondence that is known to us. However, his letters are pastoral in intent, and important doctrines only get mentioned in a pastoral connection. (We would not have his account of the origins of the Eucharist had there not been unseemly conduct by the Corinthians in their celebration of the Lord's Supper.) Paul was not averse to the image of virginity. For example, he described the Church as a pure virgin (2 Corinthians 11:2); but he did not so describe the mother of Christ.

After Paul there is no other passage in the New Testament which deserves notice. The reference in Revelation 12:1ff. to the 'woman clothed with the sun' who gave birth to a male child, need not detain us. The reference is obscure and clearly mythological, and has no bearing on the Virginal Conception.

After the New Testament

The Virginal Conception appears in the Old Roman Creed, which may be dated as early as AD 150. Belief in it must have been well established by that time to form part of the credal faith of the Western Church. What references can found for it in the apostolic and subapostolic Church?

Ignatius, one of the earliest bishops of Antioch (he was martyred around AD 107) regarded the Virginal Conception as of very great importance. He mentioned it in a letter to the Christians of Smyrna, a town in Asia Minor where had he been greeted by Polycarp, who was said to have actually spoken with John and with others 'who had known the Lord'. At the beginning of his letter to the Christians of Smyrna he incorporated a semi-credal statement to the effect that Christ 'was the Son of God, the first born of every creature, God the Word, the only begotten, of the seed of David according to the flesh, by the Virgin Mary . . .' By the time of Ignatius belief in the Virginal Conception had become well established in Asia Minor. Perhaps this happened when the canonical gospels circulated in the Church. We would expect that belief in it then became general.

It is particularly interesting to see what the early Christian fathers wrote about their opponents who denied the Virginal Conception. A certain caution however is required. Their defence of the Gospel tended to make them depict their opponents in a bad light; and we cannot be certain that they always get a proper hearing.

Justin Martyr wrote in the middle of the second century AD. In his Dialogue with Trypho the Jew, it appears that Trypho had ridiculed the idea because of its association with pagan myths such as the birth of Perseus, and because it was inconsistent, as he saw it, with Jewish expectations of the Messiah from the line of David. Origen, writing in the third century, directed his arguments again Celsus who wrote in the second century. Celsus repeated the libel about Panthera, a Roman soldier whom he alleged was the real father of Jesus. These objections need not detain us: we have considered them earlier.

Justin Martyr, however, did introduce one fresh point. He tells us that there were some Jewish Christians who refused to accept the Virginal Conception. In his Dialogue with Trypho (*c.* 48) he said:

> For indeed there are some of your own race who confess that he is the Christ but maintain that he was born a man from men, with whom I do not agree, nor would the majority of those who have come to the same way of thinking as myself, since we have been commanded by the Lord Jesus to obey not human teachings but the things which were proclaimed through the blessed prophets and taught through them.

Despite many attempts, it is not possible to identify these people.

Justin says that he was referring to 'some', not all Jewish Christians. We cannot tell whether their rejection of the Virginal Conception was for doctrinal reasons, or because they believed that they were preserving a sounder historical tradition. An early Christian who also rejected the Virginal Conception was Cerinthusc who was said to have encountered John in the public bath-house in Ephesus). His case is discussed by Irenaeus, who wrote towards the end of the second century. It appears that he was a Gnostic who could not believe that the Godhead could have anything to do with the physical processes of birth or death, so he held that Christ descended on the man Jesus at his baptism, and left him before the Crucifixion.

The apostolic and subapostolic fathers give us no real pointers towards the historicity of the Virginal Conception, except perhaps for Justin Martyr's tantalizing reference to some Jewish Christians who rejected it. We know so little about early Jewish Christianity after the New Testament period. The gospel to the Hebrews has perished except for a few fragments. It is tempting to think that the early writings of Jewish Christianity were destroyed because they were unorthodox; but this is no proof of such an assumption. We are thrown back on the New Testament evidence.

Chapter 6

Assessing the New Testament Evidence

We have now completed an examination of the New Testament evidence on the Virginal Conception. It is not easy to make a fair assessment of it. It may well have been a historical event. But we cannot simply assume that because it is recorded in two of the four gospels, we have conclusive evidence that it must be true. This is not just the kind of remark that might be expected from a liberal Christian! Those of us who have a very 'high' belief in Scriptural inspiration first have to decide whether the authors intended the birth stories to be regarded as factual history before we can begin to assess their worth as a true record of historical events. On the other hand we cannot assume that because the Virginal Conception is only recorded in two out of four gospels, it must be untrue. These two Evangelists may have intended to write up actual historical events which may have been unknown to the other two Evangelists. We must not use silence or ignorance about it as conclusive evidence that it did not take place.

Although it is difficult to rid our minds of presuppositions, it would be wrong to pass judgement on the New Testament evidence about the Virginal Conception on the grounds that we think it likely or unlikely to have taken place. We must resist the false notion that miracles cannot be true because they cannot happen. This is based both on false suppositions and on an outdated view of science. At the same time all miracles are very unlikely to take place, or they would not be miracles. God is very sparing of miracles, and we cannot assume that everything said to be miraculous is in fact a miracle. How then are we to proceed?

We have to make a judgement about the matter. The New Testament evidence is not the only consideration we have to take into account. We shall later consider genetic factors and doctrinal arguments. Here however we are concerned purely with the New Testament evidence. We shall be assessing it on the grounds of literary and historical probability.

Whether or not we regard the accounts in St Matthew's or St Luke's gospel as historically true, we have to give a credible account either of the sources from which this knowledge was obtained and passed down to the Evangelist, or, if we do not regard them as authentic history, how they developed within the required time span, and reached their present form in the gospels. We must consider the birth and infancy narratives in each gospel as a whole, and whatever view we take of their historical value, we have to give a credible explanation of silences, discrepancies and contradictions within the gospels; and above all it is necessary to determine, so far as we can, the aims and intentions of those Evangelists who included the Virginal Conception.

As we have seen, outside the synoptic gospels there is no real evidence for or against the Virginal Conception.

In the first place, we must take note of the fact that Jesus seems to be unaware of his miraculous conception, if indeed he was conceived without a human father. Whatever view we may take about the historicity of the Virginal Conception, we must give an adequate explanation for the striking silence on the subject in his recorded sayings.

As for St Mark's gospel, it is not easy to understand, if the Virginal Conception is historical, how Mary could have considered Jesus to be out of his mind near the beginning of his public ministry, and joined her family in trying to bring him back home. Mary would not have forgotten her Virginal Conception, even though this had taken place over thirty years earlier, and she may have had other children since then by natural conception. The charismatic opening of Jesus' ministry is, as we look back on these events, exactly what we would expect from such a beginning, and more in keeping with it than the previous 'hidden years' in Nazareth. However this may not have seemed the case to Mary. Had she not known her boy from his babyhood better than anyone else? Was not his present behaviour out of keeping with what he had been like? The shock of the change in his way of life from a quiet existence in Nazareth to the excitement and crowds of the public ministry, may have been too much for Mary, and she may have been expecting, like her kinsman John the Baptist, a very different kind of Messiah. She may have been persuaded by her family to go along with them somewhat against her better judgement. None the less her action in going to fetch him home is surprising.

Turning to St Matthew's gospel, his account of the visit of the Magi, whatever may be the historical foundations of the story, reads more like a folk tale than a historical record. From this story stems the Matthean account of the massacre of innocent children in Bethlehem who were two years old and under, when Herod the Great found that one of them was acclaimed as the Messiah. But Herod could not identify who the child was because the Magi had been warned to return home another way after they had visited the home of the infant Jesus. While this massacre is quite in keeping with what we know of Herod's character, it is strange that there is no mention of this particular atrocity among the detailed accounts of Herod's misdemeanours recorded by Josephus. The journey into Egypt, which resulted from Joseph's supernatural knowledge of Herod's intentions, reads less like a historical record than a recapitulation of Israel's earlier history in the life of the Messiah. As for the Matthean genealogy, this seems originally to have been compiled in circles where the Virginal Conception was not known, and the inclusion within it of a prostitute and an adulteress, although they were both honoured within Jewish tradition, suggests that the compiler believed that there was some irregularity about the conception and birth of Jesus. Of course the apparent irregularity might have been due to the fact of the Virginal Conception.

These considerations do not in any way disprove the Virginal Conception; but they do suggest that St Matthew's birth and infancy stories were primarily motivated by his desire to show that Jesus was the Jewish Messiah, recapitulating in his life the early history of Israel, descended from David and so qualified to be the Messiah, and worshipped by Gentiles from afar. If these accounts were intended by him to be *haggadah* rather than history, the same could be the case with his account of Mary's pregnancy and Jesus' birth itself.

According to Matthew, when Joseph discovered that his betrothed was pregnant, he determined to divorce her without making a fuss. As it is difficult to see how this could have been done without causing a scandal, doubts arise about the veracity of the story. St Matthew's account hinges on a divinely inspired dream, through which Joseph learned that Mary's pregnancy was of the Holy Spirit, that he is to marry his betrothed forthwith, and that the child to be born is to be called Jesus. Such divinely inspired dreams, while not unknown in the Scriptures, are a special characteristic of St Matthew's gospel, which raises further doubts about the historicity of the tale, for without the dream the story collapses. The fact that the tale is told from a purely male point of view, and the difficulty of explaining how such a source could be traced back to Joseph himself, from whom it would have emanated (especially if Joseph had died before the beginning of Jesus' public ministry) only serve to deepen these doubts.

Doubt however is different from rejection. For the Evangelist takes for granted the Virginal Conception without in any way emphasizing its miraculous nature but simply recording it as the subject of a dream which induced Joseph to change his mind about divorcing his betrothed. This matter of fact way in which Joseph introduces the Virginal Conception is impressive: it suggests that the Jewish Christian community to which he belonged had for some time accepted the tradition that Jesus did not have a human father; and even though we may doubt the historicity of the birth stories as told by St Matthew, this tradition may have been historically well-founded.

As for St Luke's gospel, even if his birth and infancy narratives were added later to the original draft of Proto-Luke, they could still be well-based historically. Certainly no good case can be made for an interpolation about the Virginal Conception in the story of the Annunciation. But St Luke almost certainly misdated the Roman Census which, according to his account, brought Joseph and Mary to Bethlehem. Unless there was a census at that time, the story of the Nativity as St Luke tells it collapses. Moreover it is difficult to maintain that St Luke, in his infancy narratives, is intending to reconstruct historical events. The stories in the first two chapters, when examined in depth, seem to be creative writing composed with rare religious insight and profound theological meaning. They show divine providence at work in the conception and birth of Jesus, they demonstrate that Jesus was the long expected Messiah of David, and they depict Jesus as the Son of God inasmuch as he was conceived without a human father. These stories, like those of St Matthew's gospel, may not have been intended by their author to be reconstructions of historical happenings so much as to body out, in the form of stories, these fundamental theological truths. On the other hand, it is hard to see how all the stories themselves could be due solely to a creative mind reflecting on Old Testament prophecies of the coming Messiah, with no basis in historical fact.

The Sources of the Tradition

St Matthew

How could these stories have originated? Even if St Matthew wrote up his infancy narratives himself, he must have had sources. He must have accepted the tradition of a Virginal Conception from the Jewish Christian Church to which he belonged. (This tradition probably existed without any attendant explanation about how the Virginal Conception came to be known within the community.) At the same time St Matthew, whether he was aware of the fact or not, made use in his genealogy of a source which suggested a very different tradition, according to which Jesus was conceived by Mary with Joseph as his father during the period of their betrothal before their marriage.

If this were the case, it is not difficult to reconstruct how this tradition which underlay his genealogy came to be superseded by the tradition of the Virginal Conception. It must have been considered unseemly that he who had been declared Son of God had been conceived out of wedlock by a human father. As belief in the divine nature of Christ became more deeply established, there was a tendency to push back the time when that nature was openly recognized. According to Paul, this took place at the Resurrection. He was 'made of the seed of David according to the flesh and declared to be the Son of God with power, according to the spirit of holiness, by the Resurrection from the dead' (Romans 1:3f.). This open acknowledgement of his divinity was brought forward to his baptism, when 'there came a voice from heaven saying, Thou art my son in whom I am well pleased' (Mark 1:11). The disclosure of Jesus' divine nature was then brought forward even earlier, to the time of his conception; and so St Matthew describes it as revealed to Joseph in a dream.

St Matthew believed in the truth of his Church's tradition about the Virginal Conception, and he decided to controvert what he regarded as the false story about an irregularity concerning this. And so he wrote up his own account of it, telling how Joseph changed his mind about the Virginal Conception when he learned about it through a dream. In this way he was able to show that Jesus was both Son of God and also Son of David. Knowing about Herod's atrocities, he introduced the story of the massacre at Bethlehem in such a way as to show that Jesus, in going down to Egypt, was recapitulating the history of Israel. Knowing of a widespread prophecy in the ancient world, he incorporated this into his account of a popular tale about Eastern sages coming to find the Chosen One. He had to show how Nazareth rather than Bethlehem became the family home, and the return of the Holy Family from Egypt gave him the opportunity to do this. To the modern mind all this seems like fabrication. But it would not have been so regarded in Matthew's milieu. On the contrary *haggadah* was an acknowledged way of bodying out religious truth. If this is what Matthew intended, we are justified today in reading these stories as Matthew intended them to be read.

St Luke

What of St Luke? He too must have depended upon sources. We have to consider how these may have originated, and how they could have come to his knowledge. He could certainly not have borrowed them from Jewish or pagan sources, for as we have seen their stories of miraculous births were very different. Since his tales are all told from a woman's point of view, it seems likely that women were his source. The four daughters of Philip the Evangelist at Caesarea, in whose house he stayed for some time, seem likely candidates.

It not too difficult to imagine how these traditions originated and developed if they do not reflect historical facts. Since it was known that Jesus was born less than nine months after Joseph married Elizabeth, it is hardly surprising that there was talk of irregularity concerning Jesus' conception. Although the misdemeanour was slight, such talk would have been unacceptable in religiously conservative circles. Old Testament concepts of spirituality identified purity with holiness, and required Mary to be shown spotless if she were to be honoured by becoming the ark in whom was the very presence of God himself. These views are likely to have appealed strongly to charismatic women like the four daughters of Philip. The only kind of irregularity which was acceptable was that Mary conceived without the agency of a human father. There was plenty of time for such a tradition to grow up after Mary's death. And so there grew up the tradition of her Virginal Conception.

Luke heard of this tradition, and was deeply moved by it, and decided to incorporate it into his gospel, whether in the original draft or in a later version. He had to show that Jesus was also the son of David. But how could he show that he was born in Nazareth when it was known that Bethlehem had been his home? He (or perhaps the source which he used) had heard of a Roman census in the past during that period, although he was not quite certain of its date. Although he had no evidence that the Roman authorities ever required their subjects to register at their original place of abode, it probably did not strike him as very strange to presuppose that this was the case; and he probably didn't realize that this could not have taken place during the reign of King Herod the Great. And so he wrote up the story of the journey to Bethlehem, and the birth in the cave, and the visit of the shepherds in accordance with Jewish prophecy. He may have learnt either from Baptist circles or from early Christian circles stories about the conception and birth of John. He probably himself composed the *Magnificat*, possibly the *Nunc Dimittis*, and less certainly the *Benedictus*. He may perhaps have heard about Anna and Simeon when staying in lodgings in Jerusalem. The accounts of the Circumcision and the Purification are otherwise fairly straightforward: he would have had no trouble in including these in his infancy narratives; while he probably picked up the final story about Jesus staying behind in Jerusalem from his Christian source, and it nicely rounded off these tales by showing Jesus' own consciousness of God as his Father.

Luke showed great creative gifts and theological expertise in writing up these stories, displaying rare spiritual insight and a remarkable feeling for women's sensibilities in these tales of great beauty and universal appeal. For example, Luke probably got from his source the story of Mary's visit to Elizabeth as soon as she was aware that she was to be a mother. She may have stayed there a few months out of sheer embarrassment when she found that she was pregnant, which suggests that she was not married until she had been three months pregnant (unless her marriage took place before she went). The story of this visit (without the true reason for it) may have persisted in women's circles which Luke penetrated, and he may have written it up with Old Testament overtones as we have suggested. Luke would not have thought of himself as manufacturing false evidence by this kind of creative writing. On the contrary he was using the traditions of his day to express deep religious truths with many biblical overtones.

There are however some real difficulties in explaining the Lucan stories in this way. The account of the Visitation is the nub around which the other stories revolve; on the one hand the Annunciations to Zacharias and to Mary, and on the other the births of John and Jesus. It seems improbable that a story of

Mary's visit to the hill country to see Elizabeth would have been remembered unless there was some point in remembering it. The story would hardly have developed purely out of the Old Testament allusions which it contains. The visit could hardly have been invented to cover up the scandal of a pregnancy on the part of a betrothed girl, for the scandal would not go away when she returned home after three months and the baby was born a few months later. On the other hand, if the story is based on an actual historical event, it follows logically on Mary's discovery of her supernatural pregnancy. What could have been more natural than for a girl to rush off to see an elderly cousin who had also become unexpectedly pregnant? Again, it is not easy to see how the whole Bethlehem cycle of stories, including the Nativity in the cave and the visit of the shepherds, could have developed out of a few obscure allusions in Micah about Bethlehem, and from the tradition which grew up around this that in Bethlehem the Messiah would be born. For all the artistry with which St Luke writes, it is not easy to ascribe these tales entirely to his creative skills or to the developing tradition of the source which he may have used.

What kind of scenario then could be given if the Virginal Conception was indeed a historical event? We may imagine that Mary would have 'treasured these things in her heart'. She might have decided not to tell them to her son. She might have felt unable to speak of such intimate matters to him. She may have been very conservative in her religious views, and there are some signs in the gospels that her son, much as he loved her, had to distance himself from her when he grew up. So it is possible that the situation which developed at the beginning of his public ministry at first distressed and disturbed her, before later she accepted and understood. She outlived her son on earth, and possibly before her death she decided to pass on the secret of her Virginal Conception to some women who were her close friends. It remained for a time a secret with them. Since it was known that Jesus was born less than nine months after his parents' marriage, there naturally grew up among those who did not know this secret another very different tradition concerning some irregularity over his conception, traces of which can still be found in St Matthew's gospel. No doubt, according to this scenario, the truth about his origins became embellished in the circles in which it was known; but in essence St Luke recounts what actually happened, that Mary conceived Jesus without the agency of a human father. After Mary was dead, despite the initial secrecy, knowledge of the Virginal Conception spread, if only to counter the false and libellous story of an irregularity. It reached the community to which St Matthew belonged. On the basis of this tradition, St Luke constructed his infancy narratives. Details about the Annunciation were known at first only among the group of women among whom the tale circulated; but St Luke heard of them through his contact with the daughters of Philip the Evangelist, or from some of the other women who gave him source material. He then wrote them all up with great skill and artistry, adapting them to his purpose. Not all of St Luke's nativity stories may have had a historical basis, and this applies especially to the Bethlehem stories; but it could account for his story of the Annunciation.

No doubt other scenarios are possible; and readers must decide for themselves which seems most probable. It has to be remembered that the tradition of the Virginal Conception might be true, even though all the nativity stories in the gospels are unhistorical. For this reason a final decision on this matter must await a consideration of more than New Testament evidence.

Chapter 7
Genetic Factors

In discussing the Virginal Conception it is necessary to consider genetical factors in the make-up of a human being. In Old Testament times, people had little idea about the basic facts of human embryology and fertilization, as can be seen from Job 10:9ff.:

Remember, I beseech thee, that thou hast made me as the clay; and wilt thou bring me into dust again?
Hast thou not poured me out as milk, and curdled me like cheese?
Thou hast clothed me with skin and flesh, and hast fenced me with bones and sinews.

There was not much advance in knowledge in New Testament times. It was thought that the inheritance of a baby came from the man, who in the act of intercourse planted semen (seed) in the womb of a woman, where it grew and developed until it was ready to be born into the world. She formed a kind of vessel which provided seedbed and nourishment in which human semen germinated and grew to maturity, like the seed of crops germinating in the ground. There was no idea that the woman contributed to the make-up of the baby. So the concept of Incarnation meant that Jesus' entire inheritance was from God, but because he was a real man, he had a complete human nature as well, which he took from the womb of Mary.

The biological sciences have provided for us a more scientific account of normal genetic development. This chapter could in principle involve a very great deal of technical biological detail which would probably be unintelligible to the average reader; and in any case the author does not pretend to be a scientist. What follows therefore is a simplified account of the genetic origins of species, with particular reference to human generation. It must be stressed that there is still a very great deal to be discovered in the field of embryological development. There is as yet no adequate explanation of the way in which an embryo develops morphologically so that it grows, for example, into a recognizable human baby, with the right cells organizing themselves (or being organized) in just the right part of the body. We do, however, have sufficient assured knowledge about genetical inheritance for our purposes.

The ordinary cell of a human being contains forty-six chromosomes (minute rods or threads within the cell which play an important part in its functioning). By a process known as meiosis, the ovum (egg) and sperm (male seed) are produced with only half this number of chromosomes. In human reproduction a sperm from the male containing twenty-three chromosomes fuses with a ripe ovum from the woman, also containing twenty-three chromosomes. Fertilization takes place when the two are fused. So the fertilized egg has forty-six chromosomes arranged in twenty-three pairs, and one of each pair has come from the father, and the other from the mother. So the couple share equally in the inheritance that they give to their child.

As soon as fusion is completed, the sex of the embryo has been decided from the father's sperm. Of the millions of sperm that are produced at each ejaculation, half carry an X chromosome and half a Y chromosome. Of all these millions, one individual sperm wins the race to the ovum, and the sex of the child depends on whether it has an X or Y chromosome. Not only the gender has been decided, but also all the many thousands of traits and potentialities of the resulting human being; as Brierley puts it, 'the broad stamp of the human being, the racial features, the family face or not, blood groups, the tendency to be tall or short, fat or thin, brainy or stupid, healthy or prone to disease. With the thousands of genes involved, not only does like give rise to like, but, because of the reshuffling of genes in meiosis and crossing over, there is the vast possibility of novelty in existing family patterns.'[15]

Of these forty-six chromosomes, the microscope reveals forty-four to be in matching pairs. But in a male there is a discrepancy in the twenty-third pair. One chromosome of the pair is much smaller than the other, and this is known as the Y or male sex chromosome. Its partner is called the X chromosome, which comes from the female side of its inheritance. So the male has twenty-two pairs of matching chromosomes (known as autosomes or non-sex chromosomes) and an odd pair XY. The female has no such odd pair, but twenty-three pairs of matching chromosomes, twenty-two of which are autosomes, and one of which is XX, one X coming from the male, the other from the female. (Very occasionally males have an extra chromosome.) Each sperm (and we have already noted that there are millions of sperm in each ejaculation) contains a different combination of genes along its chromosomes. (A gene, usually in combination with another gene or genes, is the determinant of the various traits and characteristics of the resulting human being.) Every male and female has the potentiality of over eight million different combinations in his sperm and in her ovum. So sexual reproduction enables a great variety of inherited characteristics. Under the principles of evolutionary development according to which the fittest survive, this contributes to the well-being of the species.

Not all reproduction takes place in this way. There is a great variety of sexual reproduction, and in certain species some reproduction occurs asexually. There is a tendency for the genetic make-up of such species to be uniform, so that a parent produces clones of itself, as happens with some species of water-fleas (Cladocera) and aphids, and with some plants too which have lost their power of sexual reproduction. However there are other cases of parthenogenesis (asexual reproduction), for instance among the Orthoptera, which do not result in uniform progeny.

It is also possible to stimulate parthenogenesis among certain species which normally involve both sexes in reproduction. For example, it can be induced by the chemical treatment of sea-urchin eggs. Indeed, almost any eggs that are accessible to an experimenter in water, including sea-urchins, starfish, worms, snails and even frogs, can be made to develop unfertilized, without any detriment. Heating or shaking will bring this about with the starfish, while pricking with a needle dipped in blood will achieve this for frogs! With mammals, however, these techniques will not avail. Forty-six chromosomes are required to produce a human being, and to achieve this a human egg containing twenty-three chromosomes needs to be fertilized by a human sperm containing an equal number.

It follows that these instances of parthenogenesis in the natural world, although they are sometimes quoted as parallels to the Virginal Conception of Jesus, are not really relevant to it. Their processes do not apply to human beings. If Mary had a baby by means of virginal conception, that baby developed from a human embryo, and her foetus had forty-six chromosomes. If the embryo was not the fruit of sexual intercourse, there must have been the miraculous provision of twenty-three chromosomes, one of which must have been a Y chromosome to produce the male sex. These were needed if God was incarnate in Jesus of Nazareth with a fully human nature. According to orthodox Christian doctrine, he was 'totus in suis, totus in nostris', that is to say, complete in his own nature and complete in ours. Unless Jesus had a full complement of forty-six human chromosomes, he could not be called fully human.

So the question arises: if twenty-three chromosomes did not come from Joseph, whose were they and what did they contain? Our chromosomes contain our human inheritance, and there can be no such thing as a blank inheritance, because the genes along the chromosomes contain instructions for the developing embryo. If the provision of these chromosomes was miraculous, and if they were specially brought into being by God and comprised an altogether new set of genes and chromosomes which could not have had a human ancestry, it is not easy to see in what way Jesus could be said to be fully human, because he would not have had a fully human inheritance. If these miraculously created chromosomes which miraculously fused with those in Mary's ovum were of such a kind that they might actually have come from Joseph, it would seem more straightforward to have dispensed with the Virginal Conception and to rely on normal human means of reproduction. It seems most improbable that these chromosomes which would have been miraculously created could have borne the inheritance of any human being other than Joseph.

We still have not been able to answer the question about the identity of these twenty-three male chromosomes and what they contained. If through a miracle these chromosomes were derived from Mary, because the normal process of meiosis did not take place (whereby the number of chromosomes in sex cells are reduced from forty-six to twenty-three) then it would follow that Jesus would have been female rather than male, because the extra chromosome required to bring about a male can only come from male sperm. It is possible to imagine that all his chromosomes did derive from his mother, that miraculously meiosis did not take place, and that the X chromosome derived from her miraculously became a Y chromosome. It is possible also to imagine that there was a miraculous mixing of genes so that the second set of chromosomes from Mary was different from the first set, so that Jesus was not a clone of his mother. Even then we still have to ask questions about the ancestry of this Y chromosome, or at any rate that part of it which is responsible for gender, if we are to assure ourselves of Jesus' masculinity. These are matters about which we can only speculate, and such speculation needs to be done with reverence and with reserve. At the same time, now that we do have considerable knowledge about the genetic aspects of human reproduction, we must not shrink from using this knowledge in thinking out the implications of our Christian faith.

There is no definite conclusion to be drawn from this consideration of the genetic factors involved in the concept of a Virginal Conception. We cannot set any limits to the possibility or the extent of divine miracle. Any concept of Incarnation that is purely 'non-interventionist', such as that put forward by Professor Wiles,[16] does not do full justice to the belief that in

Jesus Christ God assumed full manhood. The very idea of Incarnation involves a miracle incomparably greater than a Virginal Conception. On the other hand, we dare not accept a belief in Virginal Conception if it is incompatible with a belief in the full Incarnation of God the Son. That would be to put a major doctrine at risk (Incarnation) on account of a lesser doctrine (Virginal Conception), and this would offend against the principle of the 'hierarchy of truth'. It could result in an almost Arian Christology in which Jesus is neither fully human nor fully divine.

Clearly there are difficulties in understanding the Virginal Conception in such a way that we can be confident that Jesus was fully a man in the sense that he had a fully human inheritance. At the same time the Virginal Conception, if it took place, was plainly miraculous, and by the nature of the case the precise nature of a miracle must remain unknown to us. We must not therefore close our minds on genetical grounds to the possibility that the Virginal Conception did take place, and that it was entirely consistent with the full humanity, as well as the full divinity, of our Lord Jesus Christ.

Chapter 8

The Virginal Conception and Doctrine

The Son of God

Many of the infancy stories demonstrate, whether by the use of Old Testament imagery or by other means, that Jesus was the Son of God. This is also made clear by the story of the Annunciation. It is a vivid sign of Jesus' divine origin. It makes a strong statement to the effect that, since Jesus had no human father, he must be the Son of God.

We have to ask ourselves whether the Virginal Conception is the only or the most satisfactory way in which this message could be conveyed. The phrase 'Son of God' was not intended to be taken literally. It was commonly used in the Hellenistic world of Jesus' day to designate a special or semi-divine person. It was also used in the Old Testament to describe the status of the children of Israel as God's adopted children. In the New Testament the phrase is not intended to be taken literally. God did not take the place of man in sexual intercourse, as in the myths of Greece: he did not beget a child who was literally his son, like some pagan deity. The pre-existent Son is co-eternal with the Father. In the Nicene Creed the phrase 'eternally begotten of the Father' was never more than a metaphor. It refers to the inner life of the Blessed Trinity and opens up mysteries beyond our understanding. At the Incarnation this co-eternal Son assumed humanity by the overshadowing of the Holy Spirit. The phrase

'Son of God' is used of Christ to signify that he was the only begotten Son who 'came down from heaven and was made man'. The Virginal Conception, as we have noted, is a vivid sign of the Incarnation, because it proclaims the divine nature of Christ. But for those who do not realize the theology that underlies it, it may suggest that God literally took the place of a man in sexual intercourse. For others it may not signify a divine miracle so much as a gynaecological irregularity.

Normal Human Generation a Suitable Mode for Incarnation?

The symbol of Mary fulfilled many functions in the early Church. She gave a certain balance to the Christian faith, a female figure associated with the all-male imagery of the three persons of the Trinity. She seemed to fulfil the role of the great Earth Mother of many ancient religions who brought forth from her virgin body the bounty of earth's fruits. But the most potent symbol of Mary in antiquity as now was her Virginity.

How important is virginity as a sacred sign? Would it have been inappropriate for God to become incarnate through the occasion of sexual desire, and the sexual pleasure that is the normal accompaniment of human intercourse? If God did use human sexuality as the occasion for effecting the Incarnation, this would have been in no sense the actual fruit of sexual desire, but solely due to his initiative in using this occasion for his divine condescension in becoming incarnate as a human being. At the same time sexual desire and sexual pleasure would be brought into very close connection with the act of Incarnation. People's views on its appropriateness are coloured by their attitudes, conscious or unconscious, towards sex. Peter Brown, in his magisterial study on sexuality in the early Church, wrote as follows on the Virginal Conception:

Human bodies, 'scarred' by sexuality, could be redeemed only by a body whose virgin birth had been exempt from sexual desire. It was a heady antithesis, with a long future ahead of it in the Latin church. A generation later, those writings of Ambrose which stressed the contrast between the virgin birth of Christ and the birth of ordinary human beings would provide Augustine with what he took to be irrefutable support of his own views on the intimate relation between the act of intercourse and the transmission of original sin: arguments on the virgin birth, taken from Ambrose, enabled Augustine to inject 'a powerful and toxic theme into medieval theology.'[17]

Augustine came to regard sexual desire as concupiscence, lust, acceptable only because it was necessary to achieve the 'good' of procreation. Brown describes the different attitudes of Ambrose and Augustine as follows:

> For Ambrose, the virginity of Mary has consisted principally in the fact that her body had not been entered by a male penis, and that her womb had received no alien seed; it was, for him, a potent image of a sacred boundary, unbreached by intrusion from an alien world. For Augustine, Mary's conception of Christ stood rather for an act of undivided obedience. It recaptured the ancient harmony of body and soul, in which the will was not the maimed thing it so soon became. A yearning for harmony and for untroubled obedience on every level, and not as for Ambrose the defence of a sacred and inner space against a polluting world, was what now held the centre of Augustine's thought.[18]

These are only some of the attitudes of the ancient Church towards sex.[19] Despite the recent 'sexual revolution' they are still not unknown today. So some people will be inevitably scandalized at the very suggestion that the Incarnation may have been initiated through the normal process of conception which includes sexual intercourse. On the other hand, those who believe that sexual desire and sexual pleasure are God-given gifts which need to be 'hallowed and directed aright' will welcome the idea that they have been used to occasion the Incarnation. They will regard this as the consecration of the natural sexual instincts of human beings. In fact, the symbol of the Virgin Mother, as Marina

Warner has powerfully pointed out, has had a somewhat ambiguous effect on sex within marriage.[20] It can be said to have benefited the family at the expense of married love. If it were believed that the Incarnate Son of God was born through the normal processes of human generation, this might incline people to accept that sexual love has been affirmed by this gracious act of divine condescension.

Even if it be granted that Jesus was conceived in this way, would not the Incarnation of God be demeaned if this took place through an occasion of human intercourse outside the bonds of marriage? Many will regard such a suggestion as a foul slander on his mother Mary, whose official title in the Church (from the Chalcedonian Definition) is '*theotokos*', 'God-bearer'. They would regard it as impossible that the all-holy God should send his Son into the world in this way. But the matter needs a little further investigation. In first century Palestine intercourse during betrothal was regarded as quite different from fornication or adultery. Betrothal was a bond: it had formal and legal status. It took place when the marriage contract had been signed. Once a woman was betrothed she could not break her contract. The man could only terminate it by an official 'divorce'. The only difference between betrothal and marriage was that the man had not yet taken his betrothed into his home, and so they were not living together. Sexual intercourse was supposed not to take place during this period; but it is known that on occasion it did take place, especially when the man lodged in the house of his betrothed's family, which began to happen under the conditions of poverty which prevailed in first-century Palestine. It was regarded as a minor misdemeanour, not a sin.

Must it be presumed that it would be repugnant to God to take his divine initiative for the salvation of mankind by means of sexual intercourse which took place between a betrothed couple? Even if there was some scandal attached to the mother (and the Matthean genealogy suggests that there was), does that demean the Incarnation? What, after all, could have been more demeaning than the death of the Incarnate Son of God upon the Cross, the most shameful death that the Romans could devise, dying alongside two revolutionaries? During his public ministry Jesus shared the lot of the homeless, as he himself said: 'The Son of man hath not where to lay his head' (Matthew 8:20). He made friends with taxgatherers and sinners. For whatever cause, he was conceived out of wedlock. Some regard conception with Joseph as his father as wholly inappropriate. Others believe that, far from being inappropriate, such conditions for the Incarnation could be said to be quite in keeping with God's self-identification with those whom the world rejects.

Incarnation Inconsistent with Natural Human Conception?

Are there any reasons on account of which it could be said that the Virginal Conception was not merely appropriate but necessary if the Incarnation were to take place? One of the questions raised in the bishops' report *The Nature of Christian Belief* (to which reference was made in the Introduction) was whether it would have been possible for a true Incarnation to have taken place without a Virginal Conception, that is, if it had been occasioned by normal human procreation. The passage in their Report is worth quoting in full:

> First, if it is the eternally existent Second Person of the Blessed Trinity who is also the one person of the Incarnate Lord, Jesus Christ, then would it not follow that his human act of procreation must have been frustrated by God from achieving its normal result, namely the genesis of a new human being? Secondly, without endorsing any of the older theories which linked human sinfulness with sexual generation, would not the child of human parents inevitably share our imperfect human nature? And are there not difficulties in the belief that God was able to live out his essential character of holy love in such a nature? It can fairly be argued that this view of Jesus's human origins calls for special divine intervention quite as radical as in the traditional account of the Virginal Conception.[21]

When we consider the difficulties raised in this passage, we also
have to remember that the very idea of Incarnation is bound by
its nature to baffle the human mind. If we do not know exactly
what it is to be God, how can we explain how God and man
coexisted in the one person Jesus Christ in such a way that he
was fully man and yet at the same time fully God? The early
history of Christian doctrine contains many attempts to solve this
problem. Those which failed are called heretical; Adoptionism,
Apollinarianism, Arianism, Nestorianism, Eutychianism,
Monophysitism, Monethelitism, to name the more important.
Even the 'Chalcedonian Definition' about Christ, usually regarded
as the touchstone of orthodoxy, did not solve this question: it
merely affirmed rather than explained. Traditional orthodoxy
tended to skirt the question by means of the concept of
'impersonal humanity', an idea which looks very old-fashioned
in the light of modern genetical knowledge. In more recent times,
there have been renewed attempts to resolve this major
theological problem; psychological theories, theories based on the
kenosis or self-emptying of God in Christ, theories based on the
concept of organism, and so on. None of them can be said
satisfactorily to solve the theological problem posed by the two
natures of Christ co-existing 'unconfusedly, unchangeably,
indivisibly and inseparably' in the one person Jesus Christ. In
the light of this, it is difficult to affirm with certainty that either
Virginal Conception or normal generation is *necessary* for
Incarnation. None the less, the problems raised in the bishops'
report need to be considered.

Human Personality

The first question which the bishops raised concerns human
personality. A human person, as we saw in the last chapter, is
the normal outcome of human procreation. But the person of
Jesus was more complex: he was not just a normal human person.
According to orthodox Christian belief, he had, as we have
already noted, a full divine nature and a full human nature. The
bishops' report raises the question how this could have happened
if Jesus had both a human father and a human mother. How could

the core and centre of his personality have been divine? Would he not then have become just an ordinary human person?

At first sight this seems a very cogent point. But on further investigation, the matter is not so simple. A strong argument may also be mounted on the other side. How could he have been fully human with only one human parent? How could he have been fully divine with God miraculously creating only half of his genetical inheritance? Is it not better to assume that his divine nature had nothing to do with his genetical inheritance at all? If Jesus was *totus in nostris*, that is to say, complete in our human nature, we may assume that he had a full human inheritance from two parents. If he was also *totus in suis*, that is, complete in his divine nature, was not that due to a miraculous divine act by which the Eternal Son united humanity to himself in some way which must remain unknown to us? Is it possible to imagine any way by which these two natures were combined in one person? It is indeed difficult, but the analogy of grace does give us the possibility of glimpsing how it might have happened. The Incarnation was not a mere act of grace:

> And that a higher gift than grace
> Should flesh and blood refine,
> God's presence and his very self,
> And essence all-divine.

At the same time grace does provide an analogy, however remote, by which we may imagine how the condescension of God enabled a divine nature to be indissolubly joined to a human nature, because while a person is assisted by grace, he does not cease to be his wholly human self: he is not directed by grace as by an irresistible force. Using this as an analogy it is at least possible to conceive of the two natures coexisting in total harmony within the one person of Christ, without his divine nature dominating or directing his human nature.

Imperfect Human Nature
The second question which the bishops raised concerns our imperfect human nature, which is entailed on every member of

the human race. They asked whether such an imperfect human nature is compatible with the life of holy love involved in Incarnation.

We cannot consider this objection without a short discussion of what is generally known as 'original sin'. The bishops' report makes no mention of the belief, *de fide* for all Roman Catholics, that Mary was miraculously conceived in such a way that she was free from original sin. This belief is not part of the belief of the Church of England, but it seems to be implied in the bishops' report. For if the entail of original sin is contained within our genetical inheritance (and there is no other source for it), then it comes from the female inheritance as much as from the male inheritance. And so it follows that if Jesus was free from original sin on the male side because of his miraculously created male inheritance, he must have been free also from its entail from his mother Mary. And so it follows that Mary too must have been free of original sin. But there are grave problems concerned with the doctrine of Mary's immaculate conception. How could there be evidence for it? If it were possible for Mary to be without original sin and yet have human parents, would it not have been equally possible for Jesus too, if he had two human parents? How could all these miraculous preparations have been made for the Incarnation, including the predestination of Mary to be the mother of the Incarnate Son of God even before she was born? What does it mean to say that Mary was free from original sin, if she herself was born of a human father and a human mother? Does not the theory of original sin on which this doctrine rests belong to a pre-scientific age before it was known how tendencies and characteristics are genetically inherited?

We cannot here do more than raise these questions. But for many an easier solution to the problem seems to lie close at hand. Jesus could have inherited our fallen human nature. 'What is not assumed is not redeemed.' The wonder of the Incarnation would then be that, despite the frailty of our human nature which Jesus assumed, none the less, through great struggles and despite terrible temptations, he did live a life of totally holy love. Perhaps the perfection of Christ needs to be more fully defined. When

Jesus is described in theological statements as having a perfect human nature, the word 'perfect' means 'complete' or 'full'. Jesus was fully human. According to the evidence of the Scriptures, he was also tempted as we are, yet without sin. 'Sin' here does not mean occasional thoughtlessness, which is part of our human condition, as when he is reported as a teenager to have omitted to inform his parents that he was staying behind at the Jewish Temple after they had departed. 'Sin' does not include ignorance or forgetfulness. 'Sin' means deliberate rebellion against God. If Jesus was without sin, he lived all his life with his will totally aligned with the will of his heavenly Father, both during the 'hidden years' at Nazareth and during his public ministry. 'Original sin' is our inherited tendency to succumb to temptation and so to sin. Paul wrote that 'God, sending his own Son in the likeness of sinful flesh, and for sin, condemned sin in the flesh' (Romans 8:3). He did not mean by this that Jesus only appeared to have a human nature, but rather that he did not sin and yet he had a human nature. So he could not write 'appeared in sinful flesh' because Jesus did not sin, but instead he wrote 'in the likeness of sinful flesh'. His human inheritance was compatible with his sinlessness.

The Moment of Incarnation

Those who believe in the Virginal Conception as a historical fact claim that God became incarnate at a definite time. Before the moment of Incarnation, Mary was a maiden. After it had taken place, Mary was still a maiden, but God's very presence was within her, and an embryo which became a foetus was developing within her body, so that St Luke rightly alluded to her as the ark of God. God is immanent within us all, and we participate in him so far as our creaturely existence is concerned. But God was present within the womb of Mary in a special and pre-eminent mode, 'his presence and his very self and essence all-divine'.

In the light of modern knowledge, however, the matter cannot be quite so simple as that. Presumably God's special presence began at the same time as the human life began. But when does human life begin? Experts are divided on this matter. Some hold that it begins at the time when a human sperm begins to fuse with a human ovum. Others hold that it happens some hours later, when fusion is complete and fertilization has taken place. Others believe that a human life begins when the fertilized ovum implants itself in the lining of the womb, and when division of the foetus into twins or triplets, or recombination back into one, is no longer possible. Others believe that a human life begins during the period when the 'primitive streak' first appears in the developing foetus, and the first signs of the nervous system appear. There is a continuing process of development, and it is not easy to decide at what point the 'pre-embryo' or the embryo or the foetus should be regarded as a human life.

Clearly there are problems here which no one has as yet addressed. On the supposition that the Virginal Conception was a historical event, we can hardly suppose a two-stage miracle, first when Mary miraculously conceived, and secondly when God assumed humanity. Do we then have to assume that the miracle was the sudden and miraculous appearance of a fertilized ovum without any of the normal processes of human fertilization? On the other hand, if we do not regard the pregnancy of Mary as in itself miraculous, but none the less we believe that she did bear in her womb the Incarnate Son of God, how are we to picture the moment of the Incarnation? Surely we cannot believe that God was incarnate *before* human life began? If there is a continuing process of human development and no one moment when human life begins, surely we cannot say that there was also a *process* of Incarnation? Whichever way the argument goes, there are difficult problems here which need to be addressed.

A Fresh Start

One of the most important aspects of the Incarnation is that God took the initiative in coming to the aid of mankind. He gave a fresh start to humanity with the coming of Jesus Christ. In the words of Newman's famous hymn of which a verse has already been quoted:

> A second Adam to the fight
> And to the rescue came.

St Paul particularly emphasized this new initiative on the part of God, when he compared Christ with Adam:

> For if by one man's offence death reigned by one; much more they which receive abundance of grace and of the free gift of righteousness shall reign in life by one, Jesus Christ. Therefore as by the offence of one, judgment came upon all men to condemnation; even so by the righteousness of one the free gift came upon all men unto justification of life. For as by one man's disobedience many were made sinners, so by the obedience of one shall many be made righteous. (Romans 5:17–19)

The Virginal Conception provides a vivid image of this fresh start. It has acted for many people down the centuries as a potent symbol of this new divine initiative. The question arises whether this is the only, or the most satisfactory way in which it could be communicated.

We have already noted that Paul did not seem to be aware of the Virginal Conception; and yet in the whole of the New Testament it is to Paul that we owe the strongest expression of this fresh start. This suggests that the Virginal Conception was not necessary to convey the news of this initiative. Indeed, some would say that it would be conveyed better without it. This is because the inheritance of the past bears upon us all. We all have a tendency to self-centredness. It originated in our evolutionary past, when our very survival depended on this characteristic, and also it comes from our own past, when as infants we had to be self-centred in order to survive. With this entail, we need to be saved not *from our past*, because it is carried in our genes, but saved *from within our past*. Salvation might be said to come more appropriately through the initiative of one who fully shared our human inheritance and yet was free from its power.

Mary's consent

The story of the Annunciation closes with words of submission on the part of Mary: 'Behold, the handmaid of the Lord! Be it unto me according to thy word' (Luke 1:38). Countless people have identified themselves with these words of Mary. Indeed they have become the classic paradigm of human submission to the will of God.

The saying is important because it gives Mary's consent to the actual circumstances of the Incarnation. Some would say that the Incarnation could not have taken place in the way that it did had she withheld that consent. Whether or not that is the case, it is certainly true that Jesus required very special care in his upbringing if his human will was always to be aligned on his heavenly Father; and this required a pre-eminently loving and wise mother to care for him and to bring him up.

What however is often not noticed is that, in the story as we have it, that consent is not required. The angel Gabriel did not ask for it: rather, it was volunteered. According to St Luke, the archangel said: 'The Holy Ghost shall come upon thee, and the power of the Highest shall overshadow thee: therefore also that holy thing that shall be born of thee shall be called the Son of God.' This is a prophetic statement of divine intent, not a request for human co-operation. Mary's consent, although not invited, was certainly given with a most modest and humble submission. It is said, not without reason, that without this, the whole story of the Annunciation is much weakened.

In the light of this, it is important to realize that those who may have doubts about the Virginal Conception as a historical reality, do not necessarily deny that all elements in the story are without any historical foundation. Mary may well have had a divinely inspired intuition that she was to be the mother of the Messiah. If that were the case, she would have willingly and humbly submitted herself to this vocation. It could even be the case that such an intuition encouraged Mary to conceive a child during the period of her betrothal. This of course can only be speculation, which needs to be carried out with modesty and reverence. All that is being affirmed here is that it is possible to hold that Mary consented to her vocation to be the mother of the Messiah without necessarily accepting that the Virginal Conception was a historical reality.

A Moral Objection to the Virginal Conception?

Dr David Jenkins, Bishop of Durham, raised a moral objection to the Virginal Conception in the General Synod of the Church of England, which he later repeated in print. He wrote:

> The choice of physical miracles with what might be called laser-beam-like precision and power would not seem to be a choice which he cared, or would care, to use. For if such a physical transformation with precision and power is an option open to God consistent with his purposes of creation, freedom and love, then we are faced with a very terrible dilemma indeed. We are faced with the claim that God is prepared to work knock-down physical miracles in order to let a select number of people into the secret of his incarnation, resurrection and salvation, but he is not prepared to use such methods in order to deliver from Auschwitz, prevent Hiroshima, overcome famine or bring about a bloodless transformation of apartheid. Such a God is surely a cultic idol. That is to say, he is a false and misdeveloped picture of the true and gracious God drawn up by would-be worshippers who have gone dangerously and sadly astray. If such a God is not a cultic idol produced by mistaken and confused worshippers, but actually exists, then he must be the very devil. For he prefers a few selected worshippers to all the sufferers of our world. Such a God is certainly not worth believing in. But I do not believe that we can possibly so have learned Christ.[22]

These sentiments may have earned Dr Jenkins an ovation in the General Synod, but on further examination they seem to fall short of the theological acumen and pastoral wisdom for which he has been admired.

So far as pastoral care is concerned, it must be hurtful for many

faithful Christians today, in company with the whole company
of saints from the past, to be told that they are worshipping not
the living God but only a cultic idol, simply because they hold
a different view from Dr Jenkins about the Virginal Conception.

What of the theological point at stake? Dr Jenkins is rightly
disturbed by the evil and suffering of the world manifested at
Auschwitz and Hiroshima, and displayed by apartheid and
famine. (About Hiroshima there is perhaps some room for doubt:
all war is a great evil, but a Japanese chaplain in Tokyo told
me recently that the atom bomb on Hiroshima had saved
hundreds of thousands of lives in what would have been
otherwise a very bloody and long drawn-out invasion of Japan.)
The problem of evil is a large and intractable subject. Most of
the evils mentioned by Dr Jenkins are caused by human beings.
Without freedom of choice we would not be able freely to opt
for the things of God and so embrace eternal life for which
God has created us all. It seems that God regards this freedom
as so important that he can tolerate these gross violations of
his will, and all the terrible results which ensue, without
interfering in the natural sequence of cause and effect. It is a
truth of terrifying implications that unless human beings are
free to do evil, they are not free to do good.

Dr Jenkins mentions famines; and most famines (but not all)
are man-made, or at least caused by the actions of human beings.
However, appalling natural disasters do occur, which can cause
terrible suffering. The human race has benefited from some of
the very worst of these natural disasters; for example, some
natural catastrophe, probably a large planetesimal striking the
earth, caused the death of a very large number of species, and
ended the dominance of the dinosaurs, which completely died
out. At that time the precursor of man was a small mammal,
the size of a rat; and had it not been for that catastrophe, it
seems unlikely that mammals would have developed in size
and intelligence, leading finally to the emergence of man.
However, this does not alter the fact that earthquakes, droughts,
ice ages, tempests, pestilences, meteorites and other natural
disasters can bring great suffering to mankind and death to

multitudes. They are part of the price that has to be paid for the evolutionary process which has given rise to us human beings. We cannot say that God should not have created such a process because we do not know the options open to God in his plan for the creation of intelligent beings who can freely respond to his will.

Dr Jenkins, however, does not seem to object to these evils as such so much as to God's preference for 'laser beam miracles of precision and power' . . . to let a select number of people into the secret of his incarnation, resurrection and salvation, instead of miracles which would prevent the evil effects of man-made evils or natural disasters. We have already seen that such man-made evils and natural disasters are inevitably involved in God's plans for free and intelligent beings capable of responding to his love. How could God therefore interfere with these plans by physically transforming the effects of these evils (or perhaps, in the case of man-made evils Dr Jenkins means spiritually transforming the evil men who cause them)? To interfere with the evil results of evil deeds would be to upset the moral framework of the world. To interfere with the evil results of natural disasters would be to confuse people about the natural world and to remove the autonomy which God has bestowed on his creation. But these objections do not apply to the Virginal Conception and the physical Resurrection of Jesus if these be historical events.

There is, however, a still greater objection to Dr Jenkins's priorities. He seems to be suggesting that God is 'the very devil' unless he puts the removal of physical evil and suffering in front of spiritual salvation. But the devil is traditionally understood not as causing physical suffering but as seeking the spiritual damnation of mankind. If God did not give first priority to our spiritual salvation, he would not be furthering the aim for which he has created mankind. He 'wills all men to be saved', not just an elite; and for this reason Christians have a duty laid on them to help others to come to the knowledge of the truth.

To oppose Dr Jenkins's arguments in this way is not to say

that the Virginal Conception is a historical fact, only to assert
that there is no moral objection to its acceptance as a historical
fact, if we are persuaded that it happened.

We have now considered the New Testament evidence, and
the genetical and doctrinal implications of the Virginal
Conception. We still have to consider this belief in the light of
the Church's authority. Since Dr Jenkins's 'laser beam arguments'
were directed as much towards the physical Resurrection of Jesus
as to his Virginal Conception, we turn next to consider the empty
tomb.

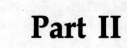

Part II

Chapter 9

The Death and Burial of Jesus

The Nature of the Enquiry

The first part of this book has been concerned with the coming of Jesus into the world, and in particular with the question: 'Was Jesus supernaturally conceived without a human father?' The second part is concerned with his manner of leaving the world; and in particular with the question: 'Was Jesus physically raised from the dead?'

We shall use the same method of enquiry as in the first part of the book, looking first at all the evidence from the New Testament, and then considering the relation between the physical resurrection of Jesus and Christian doctrine. Belief here is important, because it is obviously easier to believe that Jesus was raised from the dead in this way if he had a divine nature (although a Jewish theologian has suggested that Jesus was not divine and yet was raised from the dead).[23] As with the Virginal Conception, I will attempt to look at the evidence as impartially as I can. Before we can speak with confidence of Jesus' resurrection, we must first re-assure ourselves that he was really dead.

The Death of Jesus

There is a difference between the synoptic gospels and the fourth gospel on the date on which Jesus was crucified. They both agree that Jesus was arrested on a Thursday and died on a Friday. According to the synoptic gospels Jesus partook of his last meal with his disciples on the Thursday evening of the first day of Passover, when the lambs were being slain in the Temple Courts before the Passover began at sunset. According to St John's gospel Jesus was arrested on the previous day of the month (although on the same day of the week), and he died when the lambs were being slaughtered. There may well be theological reasons for this difference, according to whether his death or the institution of the Eucharist is interpreted as the fulfilment of the Passover sacrifice. But an equally probable explanation is to be found in two different calendars in use, the synoptic gospels following Jesus' use of the older traditional one, and St John's gospel following the official priestly calendar at the Temple.[24] In any case, this difference of one calendar day can hardly make us doubt the reality of Jesus' death on the cross!

According to St Mark's gospel, Jesus was crucified at 'the third hour' (9 a.m.) but according to John, 'at the sixth hour'. All three synoptic gospels record that he died 'at the ninth hour' (3 p.m.). Crucifixion, reserved for slaves and non-Romans, involved great suffering and usually resulted in a long and lingering death (after two or three days of torment) caused by weakness and asphyxiation (the victim had to raise himself on his pinioned feet in order to breathe). The centurion in charge of the soldiers detailed to carry out the crucifixion, and Pontius Pilate the governor, both expressed surprise that Jesus had died so soon, after only a few hours on the cross. However the description of his 'agony in the garden' on the previous night, when Jesus is said to have sweated blood, implies that he was suffering very greatly from stress; and his all-night imprisonment, questioning and trial, culminating in his scourging, would have further weakened him. Those condemned to die in this way usually had to carry their own cross to the place of execution, but Jesus was so weakened that one Simon of Cyrene was conscripted to carry it on his behalf. This detail is likely to be historical, because Simon is described in St Mark's gospel as the father of Alexander and Rufus. They would hardly have been mentioned by name unless they had been known to the Roman readers of this gospel (and Paul actually mentions a Rufus, 'an outstanding follower of the Lord', in his Epistle to the Romans).

The synoptic gospels mention witnesses of Jesus' death, in particular the centurion in charge of the army detail, on whom his death made a very strong impression. Also mentioned in St Mark and St Matthew are the women who were present, including Mary Magdalene and another Mary. The other names differ in the two accounts. The fact that these women are mentioned suggests there were indeed women present (even if there was some confusion over their names), since women's evidence was not valid in Jewish law, and the Evangelists would have mentioned them not as legal witnesses, but because they were actually present. St Luke, without mentioning any actual names, recorded a great crowd of people present, including women, who returned home, when the spectacle was ended, beating their breasts.

Is this testimony sufficient to assure us that Jesus had really died after such a comparatively short period of crucifixion? Was it possible that he had simply fainted and been taken for dead, and later recovered in the cool of the tomb? The author of St John's gospel seems to be aware of this problem, for he laid particular emphasis on an incident which he alone recorded. The imminent onset of the Jewish Sabbath, which the Romans evidently respected, made it necessary for the bodies to be taken down from their crosses and buried as soon as possible. The soldiers for this reason gained Pilate's permission to break the victims' legs (the effect of this would prevent them raising themselves by their feet in order to breathe and thus to hasten their deaths). However, when the soldiers came to Jesus, they found that he had already died. One of the soldiers, to make sure that he really was dead, pierced his side with a spear; and, we are told, there came out water and blood. Experiments have been carried out which show that this can indeed happen in such a case. (Until the Turin Shroud had been shown to be medieval by means of the 'carbon test', the mark of the spear wound, and the effusion of blood and water marked on the linen cloth, were often cited as corroborative evidence of this incident: indeed, these marks are anatomically so accurate as to suggest that they were made by counterfeiting the wound through the use of an actual body.)

The author of the fourth gospel did not claim to have seen this incident himself, but he did claim to know who had seen it; and he personally vouched for its truth. According to this gospel, Jesus' 'beloved disciple' together with his mother were present at the cross immediately before Jesus' death, so that it would seem that he was the witness to whom the Evangelist intended to refer: 'And he that saw it bare record, and his record is true: and he knoweth that he saith true, that ye might believe' (John 19:35). No doubt the author saw symbolic significance in the water and the blood. He followed up this account with two Old Testament texts which he saw fulfilled by this action – 'They shall look on him whom they pierced' and 'A bone of him shall not be broken' (such disfigurement was considered disgraceful by the Jews); but it seems most improbable that these texts alone could have given rise to the story. There is therefore quite sufficient evidence from the gospels for us to conclude that Jesus did indeed die upon the cross. His death is corroborated by St Paul in his Epistles (written of course before the gospels) and also by Peter's speeches in Acts shortly after Pentecost.

The Burial of Jesus

Once Jesus' death is established, it is necessary to determine where he was buried, if we are to examine evidence that from this place of burial his body was physically raised from the dead.

After the death of Jesus there was little time before the onset of the Sabbath when activity had to cease. According to the synoptic gospels a respected member of the Sanhedrin, Joseph of Arimathea, immediately went to the Governor to ask permission to take away and bury the body; and this permission was granted after Pilate had assured himself (by questioning the centurion) that Jesus really had died so soon. The fourth gospel tells us that Joseph of Arimathea took this action as a secret disciple of Jesus.

According to Mosaic ordinance, a dead body should not be left all night upon a tree. It was not unknown for rulers to hand over the bodies of executed criminals to friends for burial if they sought permission. As for rabbinic law, it contained provisions respecting the burial of a person who had been executed. One rule which involved *niwwul* (disgrace) was that executed persons should not be buried at once in the family grave;[25] and the court actually kept two plots for their provisional burial by relatives or officials. Only after a year or so were the bones allowed to be transferred to the family burial place. Jesus, however, was not condemned to death by the Jewish court, but by the Roman procurator, to whom these Jewish regulations would not be strictly applicable. There is no reason to suppose that Jesus' body was buried in the common grave, rather than in Joseph's tomb. However the rabbinic law does provide a possible explanation for the sealing of the tomb immediately after burial. It is possible that Jews, incensed that permission had been given for a private burial rather than interment in the plot reserved by them for executed criminals, might have tried to steal the body and place it in the public plot; but the sealing of the tomb would have been likely to prevent that.

Time was so short before the onset of the Sabbath that the tomb needed to be near to the place of execution (as St John's gospel tells us that it was). There would have been no time to move the body far. In fact we are told that it was moved to a tomb hewn out of the rock (Mark), which was a family tomb belonging to Joseph (Matthew) and which had not yet been used (Luke), and that it was in the garden of the place where Jesus was crucified (John). The traditional place for this tomb (now inside the Church of the Holy Sepulchre) is adjacent to the traditional site for Golgotha (also inside the Holy Sepulchre). Archaeological research suggests that both these traditional sites of Golgotha, the place of execution, and of Joseph's tomb, would have been outside the walls of the city as these stood at that time, as was required by Mosaic ordinance.

The Sabbath must by now have been imminent, and according to the synoptic gospels there was only time to move the body to the tomb, buy a burial cloth, to wrap it (Mark) or to fold it (Matthew and Luke) round the body, to place the body within the tomb and to secure the tomb by rolling the stone to block the entrance. (In fact Joseph could not have *bought* a linen cloth on what was by now the first day of Passover, but this detail may have been added to indicate that a burial cloth of special quality was obtained for Jesus.) According to the synoptic gospels, the women who had been present at the death of Jesus watched Joseph perform this act of piety, St Mark and St Matthew mentioning in particular Mary Magdalene and another Mary, St Luke giving a more general description of 'the women who had accompanied him from Galilee'. The synoptic gospels record that there was no time to carry out any anointing of the dead before the onset of the Sabbath closed down all activity. According to Luke, the stars were already visible; and Sabbath began when the sun set. It was however a great scandal if it should be known that a dead body had been buried without customary rites. No doubt for this reason the story of Jesus' being anointed in Bethany by a woman with a flask of valuable ointment is placed by Mark two nights before Jesus' arrest. Jesus is reported to have commented: 'She is come aforehand to anoint my body to the burying', the offence of *niwwul* thus being avoided by her anticipatory action.

In St John's gospel the account of the burial is somewhat different from those of the synoptic gospels. Joseph was joined by another member of the Sanhedrin, Nicodemus. In fact Joseph could not have moved the body single-handed, so someone must have helped him. Nicodemus however brought with him an enormous quantity of myrrh and aloes, more than half a hundredweight. The author of the fourth gospel does not record that the tomb belonged to either Joseph or Nicodemus, but he does mention that it had not yet been used for burial. The vast amount of spices could not have been intended for the anointing of the body: it must have been a dry preparation in granule form which served the purpose of preserving the body in case the customary rites had to be completed after the Sabbath.[26] Jewish law permitted a body to be laid out on sand even on the Sabbath, so that it might be better preserved. In a hot country such measures were necessary.

According to the fourth gospel, there was just time for the most essential rites: grave clothes and spices were wrapped around the body. The account in the fourth gospel does conflict here with those of the synoptic gospels, and it is more detailed. As always in this gospel, a decision has to be made whether these details are due to better information or to the vivid imagination of the writer. It does seem as though the author of the fourth gospel had access to a Jerusalem source for his gospel. In the first place, he gives a much fuller picture of Jesus' ministry in the capital city; and, so far as his last week is concerned, he knows such details as that one of the disciples was acquainted with the High Priest. Here there seems to be no doctrinal reason for the additional details about the burial other than their authenticity. Why else would we have the account of the huge quantity of spices brought by Nicodemus? St John does of course favour large numbers; but he could hardly have written 'half a hundredweight' for purely honorific reasons. Nicodemus appears only in the fourth gospel, and that more than once: he could have been a source from which this information came. In St John's gospel the story of the woman with a flask of valuable ointment occurs earlier in quite a different setting, and Jesus is reported to have said: 'Let her alone; against the day of my burying she hath kept this' which gives the story a different meaning. In St Mark's gospel, as we have noted, Jesus' body had already received its anticipatory anointing, and so according to that gospel there was really no cause for the women to return to the tomb to carry out the anointing as soon as it grew light after the Sabbath.

Before they all departed, the synoptic gospels all tell us that the tomb was made secure by rolling down the large stone to block the entrance. St John's gospel however does not actually mention this, but we may take it that the author assumes it, for he does not state that the women came to the tomb to anoint the body early on the first Easter Day, and so according to his account there could have been no reason for not making safe the tomb if the hurried burial was completed; and he does record that, when the women came on Sunday morning, the stone had been rolled away from the entrance.

According to St Matthew's gospel one further incident took place on the Sabbath itself. The Jews are said to have asked Pilate for a guard over the tomb, out of fear that the disciples of Jesus would steal his body and then tell people that he had been raised from the dead in accordance with his own prophecy of Resurrection. According to Matthew, the Jews were rebuffed, and so they themselves secured the tomb, and left their own guard in charge. The guards were present at the time when the stone was removed by an act of God; but they are said to have given evidence later that the disciples had stolen the body. It is generally agreed that all this is not historical. It is very improbable that the tomb was secured by the enemies of Jesus rather than by those who placed his body within it. The story seems a clumsy way of denying the rumour which opponents of the Christians put about after the Resurrection that the disciples had stolen Jesus' body so as to pretend that he had risen from the dead. In fact there is no evidence of any martyr's cult that grew up around any place associated with Jesus, until pilgrimages to Jerusalem began very much later. If the body had been stolen, such a cult would have been bound to appear. However the story is important in that it shows that the Jews regarded Jesus' prediction of his Resurrection as likely to result in an empty tomb, and that proof that his body had disappeared was needed if his disciples were to convince people that he had been raised from the dead.

The Testimony of St John's Gospel

In two cases, with regard to the certification of Jesus' death and the large amount of myrrh and aloes brought by Nicodemus for Jesus' burial, we have preferred the testimony of St John's gospel to that of the synoptic gospels. This raises the question of the authorship of that gospel. It is a subject much contested among scholars, in which it would not be appropriate to enter here into detailed enquiry. In the last century it was generally regarded as the earliest of the gospels. Bishop Westcott, in his famous commentary, argued that it could only have been written by John bar Zebedee, the beloved disciple. There is good attestation by early Fathers: Irenaeus in the second century attributed it to John the Apostle. He remembered as a boy listening to Polycarp (born around AD 70) who spoke of talking with 'John and the others who had seen the Lord' (a claim also made by Papias, another early Father). However this evidence has been discounted by many modern scholars, and it has been fashionable during the twentieth century to concentrate on the difficulties of this attribution, and to regard it as the last of the four gospels, a kind of inspired meditation on the gospels. And so it has often been dismissed as a reliable source of information about Jesus.

St John's gospel is certainly different from the other (synoptic) gospels, and it is not always easy to distinguish the author's comments from the words of those whom he records. There seems to have been some confusion in the manuscripts over the order of its contents, or perhaps it was in an unfinished state when its author died. There is also at times an impression of distance from the events it portrays (e.g. referring generally to 'the Jews', as though by the time it was written Christians had been banished from synagogues). The gospel was in circulation by AD 150, because a fragment has been found in the rubbish tips of ancient Oxhyrincus which can be dated around that time. So it could hardly have been written after AD 100, and its generally agreed date has been around AD 90–100. But might it have been written earlier? It is now agreed to have been written by someone with an Aramaic background and to contain material which shows detailed knowledge about the Jews and Southern Judaea.

John bar Zebedee was said to have lived to a great age at Ephesus, the likely provenance of the gospel. It might have been written by him, or it might have been based on the Beloved Disciple's reminiscences by a shadowy figure at Ephesus called John the Elder, or of course it might have been composed by an unknown author or one of the other candidates who have been proposed. But since the recent publication by the late Bishop

J. A. T. Robinson of two major books,[27] the question of its authorship must be considered open. Where material in St John's gospel is additional to that in the synoptic gospels or differs from it, it will be judged here on its own merits, rather than on the authority of an eyewitness so close to Jesus. Obviously if St John's gospel was written by the Apostle John, this would add tremendous weight to his testimony about the empty tomb and the physical Resurrection of Jesus to which we now turn.

Chapter 10

The Empty Tomb in the Gospels

The main argument for the physical Resurrection of Jesus is that on the Sunday morning after his body was placed in its tomb, it was found to be empty, with the stone rolled back. How good is the evidence for this belief?

Despite Jesus having been 'anointed beforehand for burial', the women none the less returned to the tomb, according to Mark and Luke, in order to complete the anointing in accordance with the burial rites. They are said to have bought the spices on the Saturday evening after sunset, when the Sabbath ended, according to Mark: but we are not told how they managed to buy them at that hour. Luke tells us, however, that they brought with them the spices which they had prepared before the Sabbath began on the Friday evening, although how they managed to get hold of them at the very time when the Sabbath was starting we are also not informed. Matthew merely relates that they came to inspect the tomb. According to Mark this took place 'very early in the morning' on Sunday, according to Luke it was 'at the first sign of dawn' (Jerusalem Bible) and according to Matthew 'as it was beginning to lighten' (while according to John 'while it was yet dark'). Matthew alone records the guard at the tomb, which would have made anointing out of the question, and this may account for his alteration of the women's intention (he does not mention anointing) unless he is simply following here a source similar to that which the fourth Evangelist used.

According to Mark and Luke the women went to the tomb to anoint the body of Jesus. According to Matthew they went to inspect the tomb, and St John's gospel simply tells us that Mary Magdalene went to the tomb.

None of the canonical gospels record the event of the Resurrection itself (that account awaits the later apocryphal gospel of Peter); but according to Matthew the arrival of the women coincided with the appearance of an angel together with a considerable earthquake, which resulted in the stone being rolled away from the tomb. Once again, the Matthean addition here is suspect. When considering the Virginal Conception of Jesus, we had cause to note St Matthew's liking for haggadic additions. He also has a tendency to underline key events with apocalyptic detail. For example, at the moment of Jesus' death we are told that, in addition to the rending of the temple veil (and perhaps in explanation of it) 'the earth did quake, and the rocks rent; and the graves were opened; and many bodies of the saints which slept arose, and came out of the graves after his resurrection, and went into the holy city and appeared unto man.' There is further similar apocalyptic introduced for the rolling away of the stone from the tomb.

The other two synoptic gospels agree with Matthew in recording that the stone was rolled away from the tomb, and they both also agree with him that the women saw someone inside the tomb; 'a young man sitting on the right side, clothed in a long white garment' (Mark), 'two men . . . in shining garments' (Luke), 'the angel of the Lord . . . his countenance was like lightning, and his raiment white as snow' (Matthew). All in one way or another emphasize whiteness, traditionally a sign of the supernatural, reflecting the glory of God. According to Mark, the women were frightened, according to Luke they were utterly at a loss, and according to Matthew the guards (in his account watching the tomb) shook with fear and lay like the dead.

According to Mark, the women, when they arrived at the tomb, before they saw that the entrance was now clear, said to each other 'Who shall roll us away the stone from the door of the sepulchre?' It seems odd that they should have waited to ask this question until they arrived at the tomb, for what was the point in going there if they could not move the stone for themselves? After all, they had watched on the late Friday afternoon when the tomb was being made secure, and the stone was 'very great'. Perhaps St Luke omitted their question because it seems so pointless. The very fact that Mark thinks fit to include it may perhaps suggest its authenticity. But to authenticate a remark on the very grounds of its inappropriateness can open the door to very bizarre conclusions.

The accounts of the women at the tomb differ, insomuch as in St Mark's and St Luke's gospels the women went into the tomb when they found that the stone had been rolled away, whereas in St Matthew's gospel there is no mention of their entry at all. In St John's gospel, Mary Magdalene was so frightened when she found that the stone had been rolled away, that she ran off to tell Simon Peter and the other disciple, and only later, after they had both entered and left the tomb, did she peep in.

There are therefore a considerable number of points of difference in these four accounts. Almost all of them, however, seem the kind of differences one has to expect in law court evidence from different witnesses, and naturally we find these in the different traditions represented by the four gospels. We still have to examine, however, whether this is a sufficient explanation of all their differences.

Important questions remain to be faced. The first concerns decomposition. The corpse would have remained in the tomb from about 5 p.m. on Friday until 6 a.m. on Sunday morning, a total of some thirty-six or thirty-seven hours. The body of Lazarus was expected to be malodorous when he came out of his tomb, but that was on 'the fourth day'. According to popular belief, decomposition set in on the third day, when the soul left the body. In the light of this, would anyone be likely to return to Jesus' tomb on the third day to complete the anointing? People died, of course, during the Sabbath, and their burials were always postponed until the Sabbath had ended. If anyone died at the commencement of the Sabbath, the body would have been laid out for only two hours less than the period which elapsed

between the death of Jesus and the return of the women to the
tomb of Jesus, for in such circumstances the funeral would have
had to wait for Sunday morning, as it could hardly have taken
place in the dark after sunset on Saturday evening when the
Sabbath ended. Presumably Nicodemus brought such a huge
amount of aloes and myrrh because he had in mind that there
might not be time to do more than place the body of Jesus inside
the tomb, and in that case it would be sensible to take precautions
against possible decomposition.

The second question concerns the women's visit to the tomb
in the morning, when it was still early dawn. No one would yet
have been about in the neighbourhood of the tomb which was
situated, as we have already noted, outside the walls of the city.
If the women set out to complete the funeral rites, how did they
expect to gain entrance when it was blocked by a large stone?
To roll back the stone would have been beyond their physical
strength. Mark mentions three women, and Matthew only two.
(Luke mentions not only Mary Magdalene and Joanna and Mary
the mother of James, but also 'other women that were with them',
but this seems suspiciously like an addition, just as he has earlier
recorded that 'the women which came with him from Galilee',
an indeterminate number, were all witnesses of the burial.) Two
or three women could not possibly have moved the stone on their
own. Certainly the gardener, if he had been there, could have
helped them. We are told in St John's gospel that Mary
Magdalene, when she saw the risen Lord, at first supposed him
to be the gardener. But that is very different from counting on
the gardener being present at that very early hour; and in any
case more than one man would have been needed as it was a
heavy stone.

There is in fact no satisfactory answer to this question on the
supposition that the purpose of the visit of the women to the tomb
was to anoint the body. It is only possible to make sense of the
visit of the women to Jesus' tomb at first light on the Sunday
morning, after his death on the previous Friday, if we assume
that the women came not to anoint the body, but simply to
mourn. Nicodemus' preparations of myrrh and aloes to preserve

the body until a possible Sunday anointing were not in fact needed. Although there had been no time to wash the body on Friday afternoon as custom required, there was time to complete the other funeral rites, applying the jawband to the head and wrapping the body with the *sindon* or funeral sheet. The rites had not been fully completed, but in the circumstances it was thought best to regard them as complete. The stone had been rolled against the sepulchre. Everyone had had to make off in a hurry because of the onset of the Sabbath.

The women would have been uneasy: they knew very well the *niwwul* or scandal if the funeral rites were known to have been incomplete (as it seems that the tradition behind St Mark was aware, hence the story of 'anointing beforehand for burial'). At the same time the women may well have hoped that, with the tomb sealed, the incompleteness of the burial rites would never become known. (Could this have been another reason for the sealing of the tomb?) The women had had no time on the Friday evening to mourn by the tomb of their dead Master, to whom they had ministered in his wanderings around the towns and villages of Galilee, and whom they had grown so deeply to love and venerate. They did not want their time of mourning to be interrupted by people coming and going during the first day of the week. What would have been more natural than that they decided to pay a visit to the tomb, leaving home before people were about shortly before dawn? It did not entail them in an unacceptably early rising; for it was the custom of the capable housewife to rise before it was daylight (Proverbs 31:15).

Another series of questions concerns the angel (or young man, or two men) seen by the women in the otherwise empty tomb. Are angels credible today as messengers from God? (The same question has to be asked about the appearance of angels in St Matthew's and St Luke's gospel in connection with the Annunciation to Mary, and the birth of Jesus.) Can we believe that a message so important for mankind that Jesus was risen from the dead could have been entrusted to this agency? If angels ever really did talk with human beings, this seems to be the case no longer nowadays. According to all three synoptic gospels, the women not only saw them but also heard a voice.

Caution however is needed at this point. In the first place, we cannot rule out the existence of other orders of spiritual beings besides mankind: indeed, this would seem to many more probable than not. Secondly, God can communicate with people in many different ways. There is no one single mode of divine self-disclosure. People in those days certainly believed in the reality of angels in a way which is not the case today. The mode of divine revelation is always accommodated to the assumptions of those who receive it: as the medievalists put it, *omnis revelatio secundum modum recipientis*. The women might have conceptualized divine revelation in the form of the vision and words of an angel. Thirdly the figure of an angel may have been introduced not because the disciples saw or heard one, but because this was a conventional way of describing supernatural communication.

Another area of enquiry concerns the reason why the stone was rolled back from the tomb entrance. Is it possible that it had never been rolled down to close up the entrance, and that St John's gospel, which does not actually record this happening, is in this respect closer to what really happened? In that case we could make sense of the women coming to anoint the body, for they would have been able to enter the tomb (although they could hardly have bought the spices after the Sabbath ended on Saturday evening and prepared them under cover of darkness). But the fact that the stone had been moved is recorded by St John's gospel, even if it does not record the placing of the stone in position; and so we must accept that the securing of the tomb was implied by the Evangelist, and that it actually took place. According to St Matthew's gospel the rolling away of the stone occurred during the earthquake at the moment when the women arrived; but then St Matthew's gospel had already introduced guards outside the tomb, and so he could hardly have put the event earlier than the arrival of the women, because (on his showing) the guards would have put the stone back in place and denied that anything untoward had occurred. According to the other gospels, the women found the stone removed when they arrived; and if it had been removed, this is likely to have happened before the women came.

Was it possible that the stone was never removed, but that in the half light the women mistook their way, and went instead to another unused tomb where the stone of course would not have been rolled against the entrance? We have no means of knowing whether there were any other unused tombs in the vicinity. It seems very unlikely, however, that the whole story of the empty tomb rests on a mistake of this kind. The women, we have been told, had been watching the anointing and the laying out of the body on the Friday afternoon. The fact that Mary Magdalene originally mistook the risen Jesus for the gardener, according to the Johannine account, affords no basis for assuming that a similar mistake was made about the locality of the tomb. We shall note later that, in cases of veridical hallucination, it is not unusual to fail to recognize straightway the dead person who is seen as alive. We may therefore discard this explanation of a mistaken tomb as so improbable as to be disregarded.

If the stone was rolled back from the tomb, there are three possible explanations. The Jews themselves could have removed the body of Jesus, as had been mentioned earlier, so that they could place it in one of the two common plots kept for the bodies of executed persons. However, if they had done that, they would surely have produced the body to scotch the rumour as soon as it got around that Jesus had been raised from the dead. This explanation may therefore also be dismissed. Alternatively, Jesus' disciples could have stolen the body. Why should they want to do this? It is beyond belief that they would have wished to bury it secretly and pretend that Jesus had been raised from the dead. Whatever else, the Christian Church did not begin with this kind of deceit, as may be clearly seen from the character portrayal of the apostles in the New Testament. But could they have prepared a special tomb elsewhere, where they wished to hallow the body of their Master? But we have already noted that there is no trace of any such martyr cult in the early Church. In any case, if they had stolen the body for this purpose, they would surely have rolled down the stone again, so that the authorities would not have known that it had been stolen. This explanation may also be dismissed.

A third explanation assumes that the stone was miraculously removed. Why would this have happened? We surely cannot suppose that this was necessary for God to raise Jesus from the dead. The raising of Jesus was a resurrection and not a resuscitation. We are specifically told in St John's gospel that the risen Jesus appeared to his disciples, when they were gathered together, despite doors that were locked for fear of the Jews. If Jesus appeared to them through locked doors, he would not have needed the stone to be rolled away from the tomb in order to manifest himself in his risen state outside it. But if it was said that Jesus had been raised from the dead, and that he had appeared later to others, these appearances would have been regarded as purely subjective visionary experiences, or even thought to be fabricated reports, unless the stone had been rolled away, and it was clearly seen that the body was no longer there. The rolling away of the stone must therefore be understood, if it occurred miraculously, to be a separate although connected miracle, whose purpose was to make known, when the risen Jesus appeared to others, that these were real appearances, and that Jesus' dead body was no longer in the tomb, but that it had in some mysterious way been transformed into his risen body. These, however, are only as yet preliminary considerations. Until the rest of the evidence about the risen Jesus has been assessed, and the Christian tradition of Jesus' resurrection has been examined, we are not in a position to reach any firm conclusion about the historicity of the empty tomb.

St John's gospel has no mention of any angel at or in the tomb. But according to the accounts in the synoptic gospels, the women did not merely see that the tomb was empty, they were told that it was empty by the mysterious being(s) inside the tomb. According to the Marcan account, the young man in a white garment said to the dumbfounded women: 'Be not affrighted: Ye seek Jesus of Nazareth, which was crucified: he is risen; he is not here: behold the place where they laid him. But go your way, tell his disciples and Peter that he goeth before you into Galilee: there shall ye see him, as he said unto you.' (The reference here is to a saying attributed in St Mark's gospel to Jesus speaking to his disciples at the Mount of Olives on the evening of his betrayal: 'After that I am risen, I will go before you to Galilee.') According to St Matthew's gospel, an angel spoke to the women words almost identical to those recorded by St Mark, except for a subtle difference in the angel's concluding words, with their emphasis on the angel's authority, rather than that of Jesus: 'There shall ye see him: lo, I have told you.' In St Luke's gospel the difference is much greater. St Luke does not simply record the empty tomb: he explains it. The two men in the tomb said: 'Why seek ye the living among the dead? He is not here, he is risen: remember how he spake unto you when he was in Galilee, saying, the Son of Man must be delivered into the hands of sinful men, and be crucified, and the third day rise again.'

These differences between the gospels are important inasmuch as they reflect the differing theologies inherent in each of the synoptic gospels; and these will be examined later. For our purposes here, it is sufficient to note that, despite all the differences, the words of the angel(s) in all the gospels have three main emphases: (i) that the women have no need to be frightened; (ii) that Jesus has been raised from the dead, and that his body is no longer in the tomb; and (iii) that, according to St Mark and St Matthew's gospels, there will be an opportunity for the women to be with Jesus again. In other words, if the stone had been rolled away in order that Jesus' Resurrection may be made known, the message of the angels articulates the same message.

In St John's gospel, the account of the empty tomb seems to come from a different source, and it does not overlap in any way with the synoptic gospels, except for the fact that the tomb was found to be empty, and that St Mary Magdalene was at the tomb. She came there while it was still dark, and found that the stone had already been removed. It is by no means impossible that this is the same visit as that told in the synoptic gospels, but that the other women are not mentioned by the author of the fourth gospel, because he had access to a special source about Mary, as evidenced by his telling of the story of the raising of Lazarus, which is not found in the other gospels.

According to the fourth gospel Mary after seeing the stone rolled away did not look inside (she peeped in on her second visit) but she ran to tell both Peter and 'the other disciple' (who has been identified by most critics with John Bar Zebedee). They raced one another to the tomb. The other disciple peered in first, but Peter was the first to enter. However the other disciple was the first to understand the significance of what he saw inside. (This is consonant with what is known of the characters of both, if John Bar Zebedee lies behind St John's gospel: Peter was an impulsive leader, but John had spiritual understanding.) The presence of both Peter and the other disciple at the empty tomb is in direct contrast to St Luke's gospel, where we are told that, when the women told the apostles about the empty tomb, they would not believe them, because the story appeared to them to be nonsense. (We have already noted that the evidence of women was not valid in Jewish law.) In St Mark's gospel the women said nothing to anyone. According to St Matthew's gospel the women ran away to tell the disciples and the risen Jesus appeared to them as they went. Evidently there is contradictory evidence here, which often occurs when events are remembered afterwards. Once again, we must make up our mind whether these differences are sufficiently large to cast doubt on the historicity of the event, or whether they may be sufficiently explained by different theological tendencies in the gospels (which we shall shortly examine) or by a natural tendency for different people to give different accounts which later become embodied in the various traditions behind the four gospels.

It has been suggested that St John's account of Peter and the other disciple going to the tomb is a way of describing the different approaches of the two disciples to their belief in the Resurrection. This might be an acceptable solution to the apparent discrepancies between the different accounts in the synoptic gospels and St John's gospel, were it not for one strange point which strongly suggests genuine reminiscence. We are told that when Peter looked into the tomb he saw the grave clothes lying and the napkin which had been over his head in a place by itself. Although it is difficult to understand exactly what the Evangelist meant by these details, it is clear that he attached considerable importance to them. Probably he was referring to the jawband round the head. This was away from the main body of grave clothes which were discovered in a heap as though the body had slipped out of them, rather than as if they had been discarded as a person removes night clothes when he gets up. This would account for the emphasis put on what Peter saw, and what caused him also to 'believe' that Jesus had risen.

Do these discrepancies between the gospels over their accounts of how the tomb was found to be empty discredit the historicity of the empty tomb? That must be decided in conjunction with the other evidence.

Chapter 11

The Gospel Appearances

The empty tomb on its own would have not necessarily have led to the belief that Jesus had been raised from the dead. Jesus' body could have been thought to have been removed through human agency, despite the decisive arguments which we have already brought against such a possibility. It was both because his tomb was found empty and because he appeared to people after this had been discovered, that he was believed to have been raised physically from the dead. The accounts of these appearances clearly need further investigation.

The Longer Ending of St Mark's Gospel

Most manuscripts of St Mark's gospel do not have any Resurrection appearances at all! They end with the empty tomb, at the point when the women 'fled from the sepulchre; for they trembled and were amazed; neither said they any thing to any man, for they were afraid'. There are some manuscripts, however, which include what is called 'the longer ending'. This is almost universally agreed not to have been part of the original gospel. Both the external evidence of early testimony about the gospel and the internal evidence of its contents are against it. The longer ending consists almost entirely of a summary of information found elsewhere, either in the gospels or elsewhere in the New Testament. It is also different in style from the earlier chapters of the gospel.

Scholars have argued at length about the ending of St Mark's gospel. Did the gospel really end with the words 'for they were afraid'? Was this not a very negative note on which to conclude the telling of the Good News? Or could the words imply the natural fear which is experienced in the presence of the numinous, if the women had just undergone an overwhelming experience of transcendence? But how could the gospel end with the silence of the women, when the story shows that this involved direct disobedience to the angelic command to go and tell the disciples that Jesus is going before them into Galilee? If it was to become common knowledge that the tomb was empty, how could this have been known if the women had told no one? Surely the original ending must have been longer? How could it possibly have been intended to conclude so abruptly?

These questions are easier to ask than to answer; but it is possible, as we shall see when we come to examine the theology of each gospel, that according to St Mark the end of all things was expected immediately after the Resurrection. If the women realized that this was about to take place, their continuing fear is more easily explained, and the abruptness of the ending symbolizes the abruptness of their departure.

A further problem with the gospel ending at this point is grammatical. In the Greek, the word 'for' in 'for they were afraid' is an 'enclitic' conjunction, and therefore cannot stand first in a sentence. The gospel therefore would have ended, in Greek, in the order 'they were afraid, for'. A sentence in Greek literature could end in this way, but it would be almost intolerably inelegant to conclude a whole book like this, even in the *koine* Greek of the New Testament. (There is little or no elegant Greek in the writing of St Mark's gospel: the distinction of the Authorized Version gives us today in this respect a false idea of the spoken demotic Greek in which it is written.)

The difficulty about ending the gospel at this point has led some to suppose that there was a final sentence which was removed when the 'longer ending' was added. Farrer, for example, has suggested that originally the gospel ended with the words: 'But the name of Jesus became manifest throughout the world.'[28] There is, however, no evidence for this lost sentence. In the same way, others have suggested that there was indeed a longer ending, but that it has got lost; and that some of the Resurrection appearances recorded in St Matthew's gospel originally appeared in this lost ending of St Mark's gospel. Once again, there is no evidence for this longer ending (except for those who believe that the fact that these resurrection appearances are included in St Matthew's gospel in itself constitutes the evidence).

What is the relevance of this to our enquiry about the empty tomb? It is only indirect. The testimony of St Mark, if it is the earliest gospel, would have added weight to the evidence in the other gospels about the resurrection appearances. However there is a lot of material in St Matthew's, St Luke's and St John's gospels, especially as these are (as we shall shortly see) supported by what St Paul wrote upon this subject.

The Other Gospels

In St Matthew there are two appearances; one to the women as they hurried from the tomb to tell the glad news to the disciples, and the other to the eleven apostles in Galilee 'on the mountain where Jesus had told them to meet him'. St Luke's gospel has two appearances; the first on the road to Emmaus to two unnamed disciples, and the second to the Eleven and the rest of the company when the two disciples returned and told them what had befallen them, ending with Jesus' Ascension into heaven. (A different version of the Ascension of Jesus is given by the same author in the Acts of the Apostles.) St Luke also includes a reference to an earlier appearance to Simon Peter. In St John's gospel, as in St Matthew's gospel, there are appearances both in Jerusalem and in Galilee; to Mary Magdalene at the tomb, and then later that day, on the Sunday evening, to ten of the Eleven in Jerusalem behind locked doors, and again the following Sunday evening when Thomas also was present. St John's gospel records the appearance of Jesus to his disciples again later, this time by the shore of Lake Galilee, where he makes breakfast for them when they come ashore from fishing, and where he later questions Peter about his love for him, and he in turn is questioned about the death of the beloved disciple.

None of these appearances seem to be identical. They can no doubt be harmonized with each other, but clearly they come from different traditions, and have probably been altered in the process. In particular there is difficulty in harmonizing all the Jerusalem and Galilean appearances. If the disciples were told to go straight to Galilee (Mark and Matthew) what were they doing in Jerusalem a week later? If they were told not to depart from the city until the Holy Spirit had come upon them, what were they doing in Galilee? Many theories have been produced in the attempt to answer these questions; but for our purposes it would hardly be profitable to examine them.

More relevant would be an examination of the nature of the risen Lord, if we take all the Resurrection stories at their face value. The differences found in the various stories are probably due to the way in which these stories have been shaped by tradition; but they may also reflect the changed conditions of Jesus' Resurrection life. Jesus would suddenly appear, and according to St Luke he could suddenly vanish from sight, as he did to the two unnamed disciples on the road to Emmaus when they sat down to a meal. He could be present despite locked doors, as with the disciples in Jerusalem on the Sunday evening. He does not seem always to have been immediately recognized, as with Mary in the garden when she mistook him for the gardener, and with the two unnamed disciples on the road to Emmaus, when he appeared to be a stranger, and when the disciples had breakfast with him after fishing in the Lake of Galilee. Mary Magdalene was told 'Touch me not', but that might have been to prevent her clinging to his earthly form, rather than because he was not touchable. Thomas was told to put his hand into his side, to verify that the wounds from his Crucifixion were real; but we are told that, when it came to the point, he did not do this. St Matthew tells us that the women did touch him: they clasped his feet when Jesus appeared to them at the tomb. According to St Luke's gospel, the risen Jesus said: 'No ghost has flesh and blood as I have', and he ate a piece of fish that he was given. According to the fourth gospel, the risen Jesus actually cooked the food which the disciples consumed at their breakfast after their fishing expedition.

It seems reasonable to assume that some of these details, in particular those connected with Jesus' eating and being touched, may have been apologetic in intention, added by the Evangelists to emphasize that Jesus was not a mere ghost. The disciples were clearly convinced of the reality of the risen Jesus whom they saw and with whom they conversed, but there was something different about him which made him at times not always immediately recognizable and which enabled him to appear and to disappear at will. He was neither ordinary flesh and blood nor was he an insubstantial ghost. There is even a hint in the fourth gospel, in Jesus' conversation with Mary Magdalene, that his was an interim state between his ordinary earthly life and the time when he would ascend into heaven.

The Gospel Theologies

In St Mark's gospel Galilee is the scene and seat of revelation where the gospel is proclaimed and Jesus is manifested as Lord, albeit only recognized as such by an intimate circle of disciples. Jerusalem is a dark tunnel of suffering and rejection and betrayal through which Jesus had to pass until the time of consummation which was imminently expected in Galilee, and actually set in train by the terrible events in Jerusalem.[29] The notes of hope and fear which mark the story of Jesus' resurrection in St Mark's gospel could be explained by the belief of the women at the tomb that the Final Judgement was now upon them, uplifted by the coming glory of the Messiah manifesting himself as he really is, and terrified by the fear that thought of the Final Judgement engenders. This ultimate denouement would take place in Galilee, and so they were reminded that the risen Lord goes before them there, and there they will see him as he is. If this is St Mark's theology, he had no need of any Resurrection stories according to his understanding of Jesus. His death, Resurrection and final appearing are all bound together, and all are expected to take place in a single continuum.

In St Matthew's gospel there has been a subtle change in the understanding of these events. We have already spotted the way in which the author inserts apocalyptic details in order to underline key events. In particular the Resurrection has attracted to itself some of the traditional language of the Consummation. It has come to be the focal point of the gospel. The disciples are told by the women who saw the empty tomb not that Jesus is going before them to Galilee, but that he has risen from the dead. They are not reminded that Jesus had made the prophesy of his return to Galilee 'as he said to you', but that they are to give the message about his Resurrection, 'Lo, I have told you'. These subtle changes are important. They explain why stories of the risen Lord are introduced after the finding of the empty tomb. Whereas in St Mark's gospel the focus is on the awe-inducing events of the imminent End, in St Matthew's gospel the ultimate event is actually described, and it is not the Final Coming of Jesus, but his investiture with all power and authority that takes place on the appointed mountain in Galilee, a kind of ascension scene. This is foreshadowed by the earlier appearance when Jesus met the women hurrying from the tomb. The risen Jesus orders them to tell the disciples to go to Galilee. As they will worship him there on the mountain top, so already here in Jerusalem the women take hold of his feet and worship him now.

St Luke's view is different from that of either St Mark or St Matthew. Far from emphasizing the need for the disciples to go to Galilee, he expressly excluded that possibility, with the command to the disciples from the risen Jesus not to leave the capital until the Holy Spirit has been poured out on them there. Not that St Luke omitted to mention Galilee, but instead of 'He goeth before you into Galilee' he wrote: 'Remember how he spake to you when he was yet in Galilee . . .' Jerusalem, for St Luke, was not a dark tunnel through which Jesus must pass *en route* for Galilee: it was the scene of the Lord's vindication and subsequent glorification. His role on earth was completed in Jerusalem by his Resurrection, and there only remains his glorification when he ascended into heaven; and this forms his gospel's culmination. St Luke wrote his gospel to show how the Good News of Christ went from Galilee to the capital city of Judaea, just as he wrote the Acts of the Apostles to show how the Good News went from there to Rome, the capital city of the world.

It follows, therefore, that all the resurrection stories in his gospel take place in Jerusalem and its environs. St Luke needs Resurrection stories to validate the empty tomb, because, according to his gospel, when the women told the apostles about it, their stories were dismissed as nonsense and they would not believe them. The story of the appearance on the road to Emmaus has been influenced by the subsequent meeting of Christian congregations with the Risen Jesus in Word and Sacrament, but that does not necessarily imply that the story had its origin there. The two men journeying to Emmaus spoke of 'some of our associates' (literally, some of those with us) who had visited the tomb and confirmed the women's reports about it; and this suggests that St Luke was acquainted with the tradition found in St John's gospel that not only the women but certain disciples also were first-hand witnesses of the empty tomb. This must be distinguished from the appearance of the risen Jesus to Peter before the two disciples had returned from their walk to Emmaus, and also from the risen Jesus' appearance to the disciples when the rest of the company assembled to hear about the Emmaus journey. The account of Jesus on the latter occasion eating a piece of fish was probably apologetic, influenced by the need to emphasize the reality of the risen Jesus; but, while this particular detail is suspect, it does not follow that this appearance itself did not take place. These resurrection stories in St Luke's gospel lead on directly to an account of the Ascension.

In St Luke's gospel the Resurrection, the Ascension and the giving of the Spirit are spaced out temporally in sacred periods (in contrast to St John's gospel, where they are seen as a unified single continuum, and where the risen Lord in one Resurrection appearance breathes out the Spirit and announces 'I am going to my Father'). St Luke's gospel terminates at the Ascension, with the disappearance of Jesus into heaven. During the subsequent 'period of the Church', Jesus becomes, as it were, an absentee in heaven, and the Holy Spirit (instead of, as in St John's gospel, the guarantee of his presence) becomes instead a surrogate for his absence (except on special occasions, such as the martyrdom of Stephen and the conversion of Saul, when special access is given to the Lord in heaven).

When we turn to St John's gospel we find that, just as the Evangelist follows sources different from those of the synoptic gospels, so his interpretation of the Resurrection events also differs in some important particulars. At first sight he seems closer to St Luke than to the other two gospels. Apart from the Galilean appendix in chapter 21 which was added later (for the last verse of chapter 20 is clearly intended as the climax of this gospel), the appearances of the risen Lord take place, as in St Luke's gospel, in or near Jerusalem. Like St Luke he has two heavenly visitants to the tomb; like St Luke he portrays the risen Lord as not immediately recognized; he includes the giving of the Spirit, to which St Luke makes reference; and he refers to the Ascension, which St Luke records. St Luke's gospel actually ends with the Ascension because Jesus' work was completed at the resurrection, while St John's gospel emphasizes his Ascension in different parts of his gospel. Mary Magdalene is told not to touch Jesus because he has not yet ascended. The disciples were told by him that he was ascending to his Father and to their Father. The Ascension marks the return of the Son to the Father. 'No man hath ascended into heaven save he who descended from heaven.' Despite the emphasis on the empty tomb and the resurrection, it is the completion of the work on earth which Jesus had to do which is of most importance to the Evangelist.

What then is the point of the appendix about the fishing expedition in Galilee? Attempts to show that this was written by another hand than the author of the fourth gospel have failed. More probably, from indications elsewhere, the gospel was not in a fully finished state, and its final revision was probably never completed. The appendix has three parts: first the miraculous catch of fish, second the breakfast meal together, and thirdly the threefold commission to Peter, with an addition about the disciple whom Jesus loved. The first story, with its symbolic number of one hundred and fifty three fish, seems to refer to the worldwide mission of the Church. The second story, with its emphasis on a meal together with the risen Jesus, seems to refer to the Eucharist, whose institution is not described in the fourth gospel as it is in the other gospels. The last part of the appendix is concerned with the different roles of Peter and John. Peter is to be the chief pastor, to 'feed my sheep', with a hint of martyrdom thrown in: 'when thou shalt be old . . . another shall carry thee whither thou wouldest not'. The 'other disciple' is not so much the leader as the disciple whom Jesus loved; in other words, the disciple in closest relationship to him and who understood him best, 'the disciple which testifieth of these things and wrote these things'. These Resurrection stories from Galilee, unlike those in the fourth gospel which are sited in Jerusalem, are not told directly in order to attest the Resurrection. They concern matters of relevance to the early Church: mission, Eucharist and leadership.

A discussion of the various theologies underlying the canonical gospels is important because it has a bearing on the differences in the various accounts of the women at the tomb, and in the various stories which are set in Jerusalem and its environs, and those which are set in Galilee. For our purpose what is most important about these stories is the attestation which they give to the reality of Jesus' Resurrection (which will be discussed after evidence from St Paul has been examined), and their implications, if they have any, for the mode of his Resurrection. But we must not anticipate such an assessment until all the evidence has been weighed.

The Form of the Resurrection Accounts

We have looked at the story of the empty tomb and of the Resurrection appearances in the gospels from the perspective of the two disciplines of literary and theological criticism, comparing and contrasting their differing literary expressions and theological viewpoints. A third type of gospel criticism still needs to be applied, a study of the *form* rather than the literary and theological *content* of the stories. If we look on the Resurrection stories from this point of view, two different types of narrative can be distinguished.

The first type is concise and brief. It may be slightly expanded at some points, but the additions add nothing fresh to the narrative. Examples of this kind of story are the account in St John's gospel of the risen Jesus appearing to the disciples on Sunday evening when he breathed on them the Spirit, or the final story in St Matthew's gospel of the appearance of the risen Jesus on the mountain which he had appointed, or the appearance of Jesus to the women in the same gospel when they were hurrying away from the empty tomb. The stories are told with the minimum of embellishment; and in this type of narrative, they often seem to carry the implication that the risen Jesus was not immediately recognized, or at any rate some additional assurance was needed on the part of the beholders. This form of narrative is found in the gospels in other connections, in particular in stories of healing. They have been called 'Apophthegms' or 'Pronouncement Stories' because they lead up to some saying of Jesus, such as: 'As my Father hath sent me, even so send I you.' Occasionally, as at the end of St Matthew's gospel, the pronouncement is more than a single terse statement: here for example there is introduced what has been called 'a kind of "church-order" '. This kind of story may have been told so briefly because it had previously existed only in oral tradition, and had passed from mouth to mouth, and it had been reduced in the telling as a pebble is worn down by the sea. The form of these 'pronouncement stories' of the post-Resurrection appearances has been analysed as follows:

1. The situation: Jesus' followers bereft of their Master.
2. The appearance of the risen Jesus.
3. The Greeting.
4. The Recognition.
5. The Word of Command.

The second kind of narrative is the very reverse of concise: it is extended. German scholars have called these accounts 'Novellen' and perhaps the best English equivalent is tales or stories. An account is given of some incident in a more relaxed and leisured manner, with interest growing as the story proceeds, quickened by the provision of details of what is reported to have taken place. This dramatic way of telling a story is age-old, and depends on the skill and art of the story-teller. It appeals to the imagination, and the excitement of the story-teller communicated to the hearer. The same basic pattern as that of 'pronouncement stories' can be discerned in these tales, but these are often overlaid with themes and symbols which were relevant to the primitive Church.

Professor C. H. Dodd who first made this type of analysis of the Resurrection stories,[30] recognized that there are some which fall into a kind of intermediate class, among which he put those in the longer ending of St Mark's gospel, the appearance of the risen Jesus on the mountain in Galilee, the tale of 'Doubting Thomas' and the account of Mary Magdalene meeting with the risen Jesus at the empty tomb in St John's gospel. Here too the same basic pattern persists as in the 'pronouncement stories', often overlaid by proofs of identity on the part of the risen Jesus. Also brought into this enquiry were stories found elsewhere in the gospels which critics have often thought originally to be Resurrection stories, either because of their resemblance to actual Resurrection stories, or for other reasons. These stories include St Luke's account of the miraculous draught of fishes, and the stories of Jesus walking on the water found in St Mark's and St John's gospels.

It may be noted that all these stories are remarkably free of apocalyptic detail. The form of story which is probably the most primitive is the 'pronouncement story'; but the other stories, although they are more extended and often overlaid with theological motifs or apologetic detail, yet for all their characteristics which belong to the telling of a good story also conform to the basic pattern of the 'pronouncement story'. In almost every case they lead up to a command of the risen Lord. They may well be embellishments of an original 'pronouncement story'. It is difficult to find analogies in other kinds of literature, whether sacred or profane, for these two kinds of Resurrection story. Indeed it is claimed that, while the more extended accounts of Resurrection appearances certainly contain legendary accretions the stories themselves are to be distinguished from myths, and they are closer to the 'pronouncement stories' and 'tales' of the gospels than they are to clearly mythical stories.

The reader must make up his own mind whether the differences in the various Resurrection stories, and discrepancies of place, support or weaken the historicity of the accounts; and to what extent, if any, they have been shaped by the theologies of the four Evangelists. He must also determine whether the form of the stories helps him to a decision. But we cannot stop at the four canonical gospels. There is even more important testimony to the Resurrection to be found elsewhere in the New Testament; and to this we must next turn.

Chapter 12

The Rest of the New Testament

The Acts of the Apostles

Speakers in the Acts proclaim the Resurrection of Jesus, and even, it is claimed, imply the empty tomb. So we have to ask the question: how authentic are the speeches in the Acts of the Apostles? In the ancient world it was a common custom among authors to compose a speech and put it into the mouth of some famous personage. Did the author of Acts do this? Even if he was using sources for his speeches, would he not have edited and adorned some of the material which he used and which he put on the lips of his chief dramatis personae?

These speeches have been examined in considerable detail, and there are indications that the author did use sources for them, and that he used considerable restraint in embellishing these sources. For example, there is the presence of Semitisms in the speeches, which suggest a Palestinian origin, and they contain very little material which could be regarded as suspect because it belongs to a later era than that of the primitive Church. It is held by many that these speeches represent the primitive *kerygma* (preaching of the Gospel in the early Church).[31] If this indeed be the case (and not all would agree[32]), then any material in the speeches that bears on the empty tomb is evidence which must be taken into account.

There are numerous passages in the Acts which speak of God

raising Jesus from the dead. In the early speeches there are some short summaries which seem to belong to a different *genre* from the rest. For example, at the beginning of the Acts there is a statement which seems to be a comprehensive summary of the events following the Resurrection: 'He shewed himself alive after his passion by many infallible proofs, being seen of them forty days, and speaking of the things pertaining to the kingdom of God: And being assembled together with them, commanded them that they should not depart from Jerusalem . . .'

Another brief passage occurs in Acts 10, in a speech by Peter to Cornelius. He describes the Resurrection of Jesus in these terms: 'Him God raised up the third day and shewed him openly; not to all the people but unto witnesses chosen before of God, even to us, who did eat and drink with him after he rose from the dead. And he commanded us to preach unto the people . . .' (It is not entirely clear just what meals with the risen Jesus are here being mentioned: the reference does not seem to fit precisely with any of the Resurrection stories mentioned by St Luke in his gospel.) Another brief summary of the Resurrection appears in Acts 13, when Paul addressed the synagogue in Pisidian Antioch: 'God raised him from the dead. And he was seen many days of them that came up with him from Galilee to Jerusalem, who are his witnesses unto the people.' As we shall see when we turn to the writings of St Paul, these speeches of Peter in Acts have features in common with Paul's testimony to the *kerygma* in his letters to the churches.

There are two particular passages which deserve special consideration, so far as the empty tomb is concerned. The first is to be found in Peter's address to the crowd on the first Whitsunday, after the account of the outpouring of the Holy Spirit which resulted in the disciples who had gathered together speaking 'in other tongues'. Peter told the crowd how the Jews had used Gentiles to get Jesus put to death. And he continued: 'Whom God hath raised up having loosed the pangs of death: because it was not possible that he should be holden of it.' He then quoted a passage from Psalm 16:

> I foresaw the Lord always before my face, for he is on my right,
>   that I should not be moved:
> Therefore did my heart rejoice, and my tongue was glad.
>   Moreover my flesh shall rest in hope:
> Because thou wilt not leave my soul in hell, neither wilt thou
>   let thine Holy One to see corruption . . .

Was the text of this psalm specially selected by St Luke because Jesus' body did not suffer corruption, that is to say, God raised him up in such a way that his corpse did not remain in the tomb where it had been buried? Or was the text used frequently in the primitive *kerygma*? Or did this text itself give rise to the myth of the empty tomb? This is not the only passage where this psalm is mentioned. It also occurs in the speech already mentioned by Paul in the synagogue in Pisidian Antioch. This includes the same quotation from Psalm 16. The passage as a whole deserves to be quoted:

> And as concerning that he raised him up from the dead, now no more to return to corruption, he said on this wise, I will give you the sure mercies of David. Wherefore he saith also in another psalm, Thou shalt not suffer thine Holy One to see corruption. For David, after he had served his own generation by the will of God, fell on sleep, and was laid unto his fathers, and saw corruption: But he whom God raised again, saw no corruption. (Acts 13:34–7)

Here again there is a special emphasis on the incorruptibility of Jesus' body. Does this presuppose knowledge of the empty tomb, or could it have given rise to the story? It is hard to believe that the impact of this one text could have been so great, although it would certainly lend weight to the story of the empty tomb. How could such a key conviction as that of the empty tomb develop from one biblical text?

It must be remembered that the Acts of the Apostles is the second part of a two volume work. Whether or not the Acts of the Apostles was written by St Luke the 'beloved physician', the companion of Paul on his journeys and the author of the 'We passages' in the Acts (as seems probable), clearly the book came from the same hand as St Luke's gospel, where the empty tomb had already been described. It might therefore be said that the author has introduced a reference here to what he has earlier described, rather than faithfully transcribed a text which formed part of the *kerygma* of the primitive Church. Fortunately we have evidence that is indisputably earlier than Acts and undeniably authentic. I refer to the writings of Paul.

The Writings of St Paul

References to Jesus' Resurrection in the Acts are included within summaries of the *kerygma* as a whole. The case is different in the Epistles of Paul. In his first Epistle to the Corinthians, Paul had occasion to remind his hearers of the Gospel which he delivered to them (1 Cor. 15:3–8). He quoted a statement which began in credal form, and which he explicitly denied he had made up himself. He had received it from others:

> I delivered unto you the first of all that which I also received, how that Christ died for our sins according to the scriptures; and that he was buried, and that he rose again the third day according to the scriptures: and that he was seen of Cephas, then of the twelve: after that, he was seen of above five hundred brethren at once; of whom the greater part remain unto this present, but some are fallen asleep. After that, he was seen of James, then of all the apostles. And last of all he was seen of me also, as of one born out of due time.

There is no mention here of St Mary Magdalene and the women. If, as the gospels narrate, they were the first witnesses of the risen Jesus, surely Paul knew this? Why did he not mention them? Can we invalidate the gospel stories on this account? The inferior position of women in Paul's world, and the invalidity of their evidence in Jewish law, would seem able to account for his silence about their witness to the risen Jesus.

Paul's list of testimony is not derived from the gospel stories of the Resurrection appearances, for while there are some similarities (e.g., St Luke's gospel has an appearance to Peter alone, and St John's gospel records an appearance to the Eleven) we learn only from an apocryphal gospel about the appearance to James the Lord's brother; and we know nothing at all from any other source about an appearance to five hundred brethren at once, while the appearance to 'all the apostles' is somewhat obscure in its meaning. Nor can we be quite certain just where the credal formula (if it contains one) ends and where Paul's additions begin; probably just before the mention of his own vision, although we cannot be certain.

The passage provides a different form of testimony from that of the Resurrection stories; a short bare summary of what happened, together with witnesses. Something like it can be found in the longer ending of St Mark's gospel, when we are told that 'he appeared first to Mary Magdalene . . . after that he appeared in another form to two of them as they walked . . . afterward he appeared unto the Eleven as they were sitting at meat . . .' In this case the brief list is expanded by additional detail. But the details are always factual, and there is no hint here (nor indeed in any of the gospel stories of Resurrection appearances) of apocalyptic additions. There is nothing which corresponds to the characteristics of myth, and there is no similarity with stories from the pagan world. In these respects the records can be said to have the hallmarks of authenticity.

How early may we date Paul's list of appearances? Paul himself told his readers in his Epistle to the Galatians that three years after his conversion he went up to Jerusalem, and stayed with Peter for a fortnight without seeing any of the other apostles, except for James the Lord's brother. 'Now the things that I write to you,' he commented, 'behold, before God I lie not' (Galatians 1:20), and there is no reason to doubt his word. What did Peter and Paul talk about during that fortnight? Professor Dodd used to remark, in the course of his lectures in Cambridge University, 'We can be sure that when they met, they did not talk about the weather.' We are safe in surmising that this was the occasion when the facts were imparted to Paul about the Resurrection. It is difficult to date this with accuracy. Probably 'after three years', according to the Jewish way of counting, means 'two years later'. The Resurrection of Jesus probably took place in AD 33 and Paul was probably converted in AD 33 or 34, and visited Jerusalem in AD 36. We have thus taken the testimony to the Resurrection back to within three years of the time when it was said to have taken place. By that time, according to the evidence of Paul, the testimony had already taken a semi-credal form.

Is this more than mere testimony to the fact of Jesus' Resurrection? It is part of the credal formula that Jesus not only died, but was 'buried' and then raised to life. (Again, in his Epistle to the Romans he emphasized the same point and actually incorporated it into his understanding of Christian baptism. 'We are buried with him by baptism into his death; that like as Christ was raised up from the dead by the glory of the Father, even so we also should walk in newness of life' (Romans 6:4.).) Why was it emphasized that Jesus was *buried* unless it was taken for granted that he rose from the tomb where he was buried? His Resurrection, according to the *kerygma*, was no mere spiritual experience, but rather an actual event which took place when his body was entombed. It has been suggested that the reference to burial was included in order to emphasize 'the reality and finality of Jesus' death', with possibly an overtone of the fulfilment of the prophecy of Isaiah 53:9. This is not fully convincing. The inclusion of 'buried' within a terse summarizing formula, where there would seem no room for additions to emphasize the finality and reality of his death, must surely have had a particular significance of its own. The formula is about Jesus, not about his tomb; and so a specific reference to the empty tomb would have been out of place in this context, but the fact that Jesus is specifically said to have been 'buried' seems to imply the empty tomb.

Could a Jew like Paul even have entertained the possibility of a purely spiritual Resurrection? We have already noted that St Matthew, in telling the (probably fictitious) story of the guards' watch by the tomb, shows that it would be assumed that a Resurrection would involve an empty tomb. Mere resuscitation, however, was ruled out by Paul. He wrote: 'Flesh and blood cannot inherit the Kingdom of God' (I Corinthians 15:50). The

physical body is corruptible, the spiritual body incorruptible. Paul
emphasized the spiritual nature of the resurrection body. There
is a continuity between it and the physical body, like that between
grain and the seed from which it springs. 'It is sown a natural
body: it is raised a spiritual body' (I Corinthians 15:44). Paul did
not say here that the one body is quite a different organism from
the other: on the contrary, the one grows out of the other. The
earthly body does not disappear so that we change it for another,
heavenly, body. There is a transformation of the earthly into the
spiritual, when 'we shall all be changed, in a moment, in the
twinkling of an eye, at the last trump' (I Corinthians 15:51f.). So
it was with Christ (in advance of the general resurrection); so it
will be also with Christ's at his coming.

Paul discussed the resurrection body again in his second letter
to the Corinthians. Here indeed he did speak of what happens
when 'our earthly house of this tabernacle dissolved' (2
Corinthians 5:1). (There are those who think that this passage
refers to the Church as the body of Christ; but the easiest
interpretation concerns the destiny of the human body.) Even
here Paul could not envisage a putting off of the earthly body
so much as the putting on of the heavenly body: 'We that are
in this tabernacle do groan, being burdened: not for that we
would be unclothed, but clothed upon, that mortality might be
swallowed up of life. Now he that hath wrought us for the self
same thing is God, who also hath given unto us the earnest of
the Spirit' (2 Corinthians 5:4f.). Paul obviously had thought
deeply on this matter. He was disinclined to cast off the old Jewish
idea that resurrection meant renewal of earthly life, and he
managed to retain this by the concepts of 'putting on' and
'transformation', as when he wrote that Christ 'will change our
vile body, that it may be fashioned like unto his glorious body'
(Philippians 3:21). The Resurrection of Jesus as told in the gospels
is entirely consonant with this concept, involving the
transformation of Jesus' material body into his Resurrection body
and later – so it seems – his Resurrection body into his body
of glory. For Paul a person after death was never to be thought
of as naked (i.e. pure spirit) but always 'clothed upon'.

In the fifteenth chapter of his First Epistle to the Corinthians Paul has left us in no doubt about the importance of all this:

> If there be no resurrection of the dead, then is Christ not risen; and if Christ be not risen, then is our preaching vain, and your faith is also vain. Yea, and we are also found false witnesses of God; because we have testified of God that he raised up Christ whom he raised not up, if so be that the dead rise not (I Corinthians 15:13ff.).

Evidently for Paul the truth of the Resurrection is cardinal to the Christian faith. We cannot be certain that Paul knew about the empty tomb; although if it was a fact, it is almost beyond belief that Peter did not tell him about it when he stayed with him for a fortnight in AD 36 or thereabouts. If he did know about it, he had no particular need to refer to it in any of these passages in his extant letters. The idea of the empty tomb is entirely consonant with his views about resurrection, and the reference in his semi-credal form of the *kerygma* to 'buried' as well as 'dead' may be taken as suggesting that he probably did know of it.

St Paul's Conversion

There is one further matter which needs to be examined in connection with Paul's belief in the physical Resurrection of Jesus. He added himself to the list of witnesses in his letter to the Corinthians, completing his testimony with the words: 'Last of all he was seen of me also . . .' We know from the Acts of the Apostles that there was no physical appearance of the risen Jesus at the time of Paul's conversion. No less than three accounts of the event are given; and it seems strange that the author should have used up precious space in his manuscript with three accounts of the same event unless he regarded it as of cardinal importance, and also unless he was relying on three different sources. The difference of sources would account for the minor differences in these various accounts.

In the author's primary account in Acts 9, Paul saw a bright light, which temporarily blinded him, and heard a voice. Those with him also heard a voice but saw no one. When Paul spoke to the crowd after the temple riot which led to his arrest, he spoke of his conversion. He said he had seen a bright light and heard a voice, but according to this account those with him only saw the light (Acts 22:9). Later, when Paul spoke before Agrippa at Caesarea, he is reported to have repeated that he and his companions saw a bright light and he heard a voice (Acts 26:13f.). In all three cases the voice is that of Jesus whom he is accused of persecuting by his attacks on the Christian Church. There is thus excellent evidence that Paul, on his conversion, did not see the figure of the risen Jesus. His was a vision of light and the sound of a voice, an entirely non-physical experience. If he joined this account of his vision to the previous testimonies about the Resurrection of Jesus, does it not follow that all the other appearances in his list were also visionary (or hallucinatory)? He admitted, however, that there was something odd about his conversion. It took place much later than the other Resurrection appearances, so that it was like an untimely birth. But he had to mention his own experience alongside the others, because an experience of the risen Jesus was prerequisite for an apostle; and although he was 'the least of all the apostles because he persecuted the Church of God', yet he was an apostle, and possessed the credentials of an apostle by virtue of this vision.

Paul was a man of strong feelings and deep religious experience. He told the Corinthians, for example, that he was more gifted in ecstatic utterance than any of them, a strong statement to make in the light of the problems that glossolalia (speaking in tongues) had brought to that church assembly. We are told in the Acts of the Apostles of other visions of Jesus which he enjoyed; and they are recounted without embellishment in an almost matter-of-fact way. In his speech to the crowd after his arrest in Jerusalem, Paul told them that, after his conversion, when he returned to Jerusalem, he fell into a trance during prayer, and 'saw him' speaking to him (Acts 22:18), and the risen Jesus ordered him to leave Jerusalem. Again, when he was in Corinth and meeting with opposition, one night the Lord appeared to him in a vision (Acts 18:9), and told him to go on with his preaching, which he did for some eighteen months. Again, after he had been arrested by the Roman authorities after the near-riot in the Temple, and had next day addressed the Sanhedrin, that night the Lord appeared to him, strengthening his resolve, and prophesying to him that he would give his witness in Rome itself (Acts 23:11). Presumably it was on the strength of this vision that Paul later appealed to Caesar.

Paul did not appeal to these visionary experiences in his writings. He almost apologized for being forced to mention them. 'It is not expedient for me doubtless to glory. I will come to visions and revelations of the Lord' (2 Corinthians 12:1). As a matter of fact in this passage he only mentioned one such vision because he did not want his readers to judge him except by the evidence of their own eyes and ears. The vision that he did recount is remarkable enough. 'I know a man in Christ above fourteen years ago (whether in the body I cannot tell; or whether out of the body I cannot tell; God knoweth;) such an one caught up into the third heaven. And I knew such a man (whether in the body or out of the body, I cannot tell: God knoweth;) how that he was caught up into paradise, and heard unspeakable words, which it is not lawful for a man to utter' (2 Corinthians 12:2–4). In the same passage he also recounted how God once answered his prayer directly with the words: 'My grace is sufficient for thee' (2 Corinthians 12:9).

Clearly Paul had a very rich spiritual life which he preferred to keep to himself, itself a mark of its authenticity. It is not easy to relate these later visions to that of his initial conversion, except to note that religious experience came very naturally to him. Certainly before his conversion he was under considerable stress, harrying the Church, and under such a strong feeling of compulsion that he was making journeys in foreign lands to persecute Christians. We shall note later that this psychological state is one that is more susceptible to subjective hallucination than others. It could be that this state of mind acted as a trigger to a pent up subconscious feeling of attraction to Christ which he had repressed, and the result was his persecution complex. At last the stress was too great, and the result was his conversion experience; and the strength of mind with which he had expressed his feelings came out in the vigour of this experience which temporarily blinded him. On the other hand, it could be that Paul heard words and saw a bright light as a result of Christ's presence breaking directly into his life, so that this was a veridical hallucination. (We shall discuss subjective and veridical hallucination later.)

Paul used the Greek word *ophthe* to describe his visionary experience, and he also used it to describe the other appearances in his list. *Ophthe* was a word used for visions, as well as for direct ordinary sight. If we conclude that what Paul saw and heard was real enough to his experience, but not something that would have been recorded by a camera or a tape recorder (indeed, those with him did not in all the accounts hear the words which Paul heard), then must we not also say the same of the other witnesses whom Paul cited? Further, if this were the case, would this not be the most likely explanation underlying the Resurrection appearances in the gospels? On the other hand they might have been different in kind, even if Paul did not distinguish them from his own. At least there is no good reason in the text for supposing that Paul thought that his vision was in any way inferior to the other appearances of Jesus, apart from the fact that it was later, like an untimely birth, because he had persecuted the Church of Christ. Nor, as we shall see, is Paul's witness inconsistent with the empty tomb, although it does not require it.

The New Testament Understanding of the Resurrection

If Jesus' Resurrection had been purely spiritual and not physical, and if therefore the story of the empty tomb is either legendary or fabricated, could there have been doctrinal reasons for the development of this story as a myth symbolizing the objective reality of Jesus' Resurrection? We have not yet reached the point of deciding whether or not the story is genuine; we are merely considering whether there could have been doctrinal considerations which might have brought it into being.

First, it is necessary to see the theological significance given to the Resurrection in the New Testament, and to enquire whether this could have influenced the development of a myth about the empty tomb. We have already considered the different theologies underlying the four gospel accounts of Jesus' Resurrection. However, the stories about the Resurrection appearances are much older than the composition of the gospels, so that the differing theology underlying each gospel could not have given rise to the stories. We have to look elsewhere in the New Testament, in the Acts of the Apostles and in the writings of Paul, to discover the theology of Resurrection as this was understood in the primitive Church.

In the Acts, the summary of the primitive *kerygma* asserted the fact of Jesus' Resurrection, without giving any interpretation to it as Paul did (e.g., 'delivered for our offenses and raised for our justification' (Romans 4:25)). None the less the theme of vindication is not far from the surface, as when Peter said to an afternoon crowd in the Temple shortly after the Resurrection: 'Ye denied the Holy One and the Just, and desired a murderer to be granted you; and killed the Prince of life, whom God hath raised from the dead; whereof we are witnesses' (Acts 3:14f.). In another passage the idea is expressed that Jesus was too powerful to be kept prisoner by death − 'Whom God raised up, having loosed the pangs of death, because it was not possible that he should be holden of it' (Acts 2:24). While physical Resurrection certainly heightens the vindication which Jesus received at his Father's hands, it could not be said exactly to require it.

More important are Peter's proclamations that 'God has made the Jesus whom you crucified both Lord and Messiah' (Acts 2:36) and 'Him hath God exalted with his right hand to be a Prince and a Saviour' (Acts 5:31). If Jesus here had been regarded as Messiah during his earthly existence, this would not have suggested a physical Resurrection, for God could have taken the Messiah straight to heaven. But if it was his Resurrection itself which marked Jesus as Messiah, as the texts seem to suggest, that is another matter. It was certainly common belief that the Messiah would come to earth in physical form, although it must be admitted that there was much confusion of ideas in first-century Palestine on this subject. However there are hints in the gospels that Jesus was indeed recognized as the 'hidden Messiah' during his earthly lifetime; and so it is unlikely that the idea of the empty tomb could have arisen on this account. So far as the second text cited above is concerned, the idea of exaltation (lifting up into heaven) does not in itself require a physical resurrection, for 'flesh and blood cannot inherit the Kingdom of Heaven'. In another passage, Paul, when speaking in Athens on the Areopagus, connected the resurrection with judgement day: God 'hath appointed a day, in the which he will judge the world in righteousness by that man whom he hath ordained; whereof he hath given assurance unto all men, in that he hath raised him from the dead' (Acts 17:31). That assurance could well include the idea of physical resurrection; but the Resurrection of Jesus seems more likely to have given rise to Paul's assurance about judgement day rather than the other way round.

What of the writings of Paul himself? He begins his Epistle to the Romans somewhat formally writing that Jesus was 'declared to be Son of God with power, according to the spirit of holiness, by the resurrection from the dead' (Romans 1:4). It is doubtful whether the story of the empty tomb could have come into existence simply because of the belief that the risen Jesus was Son of God. This belief is implicit during his lifetime, as can be seen by his use of the text: 'The Lord said to my Lord: sit thou on my right hand . . .' (Mark 12:36). The 'mighty act' whereby Jesus was raised is emphasized in the Epistle to the Ephesians: '. . . according to the working of his mighty power, which he wrought in Christ, when he raised him from the dead' (Ephesians 1:19f.). Just as Jesus, according to Paul, was declared Son of God by his Resurrection, so also, he told the Philippians, 'God raised him to the heights and gave him the name above all names.' This however seems to refer to his exaltation into heaven, rather than to his Resurrection, and it could hardly have given rise to a story about an empty tomb.

Is it possible to find the origin for the belief in the empty tomb in the parallels which Paul drew between the Resurrection of

the matter of which we are composed has been ordered in a very complex and wonderful way, so that we are able to renew our cells, ingest nourishment and get rid of waste matter, and thus maintain our ability to continue living – until death intervenes. Then we come not to a colon or semi-colon, but to a full stop. Fortunately we have evolved the ability to reproduce ourselves, so that our genes can live on in others, but we ourselves are no more.

If God is God, it is possible that we could come to a full stop, but he could recreate us again out of nothing, so that there would still be a real continuity between what we were and what we shall be. In such a case he may be said to have resurrected us with a new body which corresponds to the old body in such a way that there is a continuity of personality. If all things are possible for God, then resurrection of this kind must surely be possible.

This method of resurrection, however, may seem to us a very strange one. It suggests that God might have made a better job of creating human beings if it is necessary for them to come to a complete end until, by an astonishing miracle, he reconstitutes out of nothing each human being in a new form with a new and immaterial kind of body.

The idea of an immortal soul being imprisoned during this life inside an earthly body has always been popular among those who regard the material world as an inferior creation; but such a view is in conflict with the Christian belief that the material creation which God has made was seen by him as 'very good'. Christians have rejected the idea of spirit imprisoned in matter, and they have found it very difficult to accept the concept of total annihilation at death followed by re-creation *ex nihilo*. They have commonly believed that God has created human beings a unity of body and soul; and that, after the body has died, the soul remains in limbo, until it is clothed with a new body. The situation is somewhat similar to the software of a computer when software is no longer embodied in its hardware. If hardware of another kind is provided (a spiritual body), and the software is embodied in this, a person may be said to be 'raised from the dead' and to come to life in this new medium, with a continuity between his new and his old body. (The computer analogy is by no means exact, but it serves to illustrate the idea of an embodied soul.) A body of some kind is needed for active personality: otherwise a person would be entirely passive and unable to communicate with or relate to others. Our Creator could appropriately be credited with such a design, since it in no way diminishes the glory of the earthly body which he has created nor does it denigrate the wonderful way in which it has evolved. At the same time it leaves the door open from our present world to the next, with the prospect of a yet more glorious body in the world to come.

In talking in this way about resurrection, we speak of things which are mysterious and unknown. It could be that God has so arranged matters that this life is the only life, because he knows that this is best for our welfare. But if he has enabled us to evolve so that we may have communion with him, another form of life after we die would seem appropriate for the furtherance of this communion, if this is the end for which he has created us. In any case, we are so frail and foolish and fault-ridden in this life that God's experiment in effecting the evolution of life into intelligent beings would seem to be a failure if there were no chance of further development after death. And if his nature is pure love, it would seem inappropriate that he would acquiesce in such a failure, but rather prepare the way further for our eternal communion with himself. For those who believe in God, resurrection is a very reasonable faith.

Reasons for Accepting Jesus' Resurrection

Jesus' resurrection, however, is different. Christian people down the ages and all over the world are aware of his continuing life, and the difference that this makes to their own lives. They believe that in a real sense they actually participate in his life. Belief in the Resurrection of Jesus would not have flourished had this not been part of the spiritual experience of Christian believers down the centuries. Of course they could be mistaken. That is a problem which all must face who rely only on religious experience for the confirmation of their faith. None the less it is a very strong factor which needs to be taken into account (and indeed to be explained away) by all those who do not believe that Jesus has been raised from the dead.

There are however other important reasons for believing in the Resurrection of Jesus apart from personal experience. An explanation must be given for the very existence of the primitive Church. How could it have come into existence, if Jesus had not risen from death? When Jesus was crucified, his disciples all forsook him and fled. There is no good reason to doubt the truth of this statement in the gospels. Their hopes were shattered. They had expected him to bring about the transformation of Israel and the establishment of God's Kingdom. They had confidently hoped that he would bring to an end the present order of existence in the world. But Jesus was put to death like a common criminal, and the world just went on going on. Although the disciples had often been warned by Jesus that things would turn out very differently from the way which they expected, they seem to have taken no notice of what he said. And when Jesus died, his movement was broken. People had applauded him when he rode into the capital city on a donkey to signify a humble Messiah, and they cried out 'Hosanna' in their praise. But less than a week later we are told that the crowds shouted out 'Crucify him' and preferred that a robber should be spared rather than Jesus. We cannot be sure about the detailed historical accuracy of the account of his last week on earth, but we have no reason to doubt its general veracity.

On the Sunday after Jesus' death the previous Friday his small band of followers were transformed. This was no sudden 'flash in the pan'; their changed state continued. Instead of being abject and downcast, they were confident and cheerful. They were convinced that he whom they had thought of as God-forsaken had actually been vindicated by God. One of their main characteristics is called in the Greek *parresia*, that is to say, an ability to speak forthrightly with openness and confidence. They were even prepared to assert in public that the authorities had put to death by the cruellest and most ignominious form of

execution him whom God had chosen to be the nation's Messiah
or Saviour. There must have been some reason for this sudden
and continuing change. According to our records, it is because
they were convinced that Jesus had risen from the dead, and had
actually appeared to them in person. Not only had he appeared,
but he had given them orders about what they must do. He whom
the world had considered a failure and an object of derision and
contempt had shown himself to be glorified and vindicated by
the very process which the world had regarded as proof of his
failure. He promised his disciples a strength and a power which
was more than their own, or which at any rate seemed beyond
their human abilities; and his promise came true. Their assurance
about the reality of his Resurrection can provide us with an
adequate explanation of their sudden change of mood which gave
them such renewal and confidence, for which no other
psychological explanations would seem to suffice. And then –
if we accept the story of the empty tomb – they had additional
assurance in an objective sign of his Resurrection from the dead.

This is a powerful case. However we must consider whether
there are any naturalistic explanations which can satisfactorily take
the place of what seemed to them clearly an act of God.
Explanations need to be twofold; first, in connection with the
Resurrection appearances, and secondly in connection with the
empty tomb.

The Experienced Reality

Those who do not believe in God are very unlikely to accept the
reality of the Resurrection appearances, and members of other
faiths are disinclined to accept them. The appearances are not
universally accepted as historically true by those who call
themselves Christians. There are those who believe that there is
no life other than our earthly existence. The most we can hope
for is to be held in the memory of God. Others have said that
eternal life consists in sharing the divine view of one's earthly
existence. Others have suggested that eternal life is simply the
moral quality of one's present life. According to Rudolf Bultmann,

the Easter event is reduced to a decision on our part to accept the Christ who meets us in the Easter preaching of the Church, so that the question whether these events are true or not is irrelevant to faith. People who hold such views do not accept the Resurrection appearances as historically true.

It has been held by some that the stories of the Resurrection appearances were told to embody the truth that despite appearances (e.g. the crucifixion) good always conquers evil in the end. The whole Easter story then becomes a kind of parable showing the supreme value of self-sacrificing love, superior to all other human attitudes. Although by the Crucifixion the enemies of Jesus put an end to his physical life, they could not bring an end to his spiritual influence, which has grown down the ages. His memory still inspires people to noble attitudes of mind, it incites them to great deeds of love, and it fills them with hope for the future. Those who think that the Christian faith is simply an 'agapeistic way of life' (that is to say, living in such a way that self-sacrificing life predominates) will be bound to think of the event of Easter and the stories of the Easter appearances as myths, important because they inculcate this 'agapeistic attitude', but without historical foundations.

It is impossible to disprove this kind of interpretation of Jesus' Resurrection, because neither proof nor disproof is possible in this area; but it is possible to show it is improbable. In the first place, it does not account for the remarkable change of attitude on the part of the disciples after the Crucifixion of Jesus. Dostoevsky, in his novel *The Idiot* described a painting of Jesus' death as a result of which he meditated on the impact of that death on his disciples:

In the picture the face is terribly smashed with blows, swollen, covered with terrible, swollen and bloodstained bruises, the eyes open and squinting; the large open whites have a sort of dead and glassy glint. But, strange to say, as one looks at the dead body of this tortured man, one cannot help asking oneself the peculiar and interesting question: if such a corpse (and it must have been like that) had been seen by his disciples, by his future chief apostles, by all who followed him and worshipped him, how then could they possibly have believed as they looked at that corpse that that martyr could rise again? . . . The people surrounding the dead man must have been overwhelmed by a feeling of terrible anguish and dismay on that evening that had shattered all their hopes and almost all their beliefs at one fell blow. They must have parted in a state of most dreadful terror . . .[34]

Those who reject the Resurrection stories are under an obligation to explain how, without such appearances, there was such an abrupt change of mood on the part of the disciples, from despondency to joy, from despair to expectation and hope. How did this body of men and women become convinced, after the sight of this beaten and crucified corpse which was evidently so very dead, that Jesus was alive? Something must have occurred to make such a tremendous psychological impact on them that it caused this abrupt change of mood.

Those who reject Jesus' Resurrection find a naturalistic explanation very difficult to achieve, especially as the accounts of Jesus' Resurrection appearances are soberly narrated, without the apocalyptic touches which we might expect in a legendary or fabricated account. Moreover, the form of the stories, far from militating against their veracity, tends to support it. Only those details which have an obvious apologetic motive may be regarded as inauthentic in their present form. In considering the differing theologies underlying the various gospel accounts of the burial and Resurrection, we have concluded that these theologies cannot account for the stories themselves, only for some of the differences between the stories in the different gospels. It is true that there is a difficulty over location and timing which prevent us from putting together the Resurrection stories as a consistent whole. We have insufficient evidence to know the real course of events immediately after the Resurrection. But these differences cannot easily be held to invalidate the actual appearances in the stories: they are more like difficulties which we encounter in putting them together, and in deciding details of veracity and embellishment. They are not even the earliest evidence for the Resurrection. The summaries in Acts seem to belong to very early Christian tradition, with parallels in the Pauline letters; and of course there is the earliest witness of all, Paul, whose testimony takes us back to within a very few years of the Resurrection event itself.

If these stories are based on reality, we still have to determine the nature of this reality. Were the appearances of Jesus to his disciples subjective visions, or were they objective realities? As we might put it today, 'Was there anybody there?' Were they real experiences which had no basis in reality? Various explanations are possible.

(1) Objective Appearances

It is possible to regard the appearances of Jesus as objectively real appearances, in the sense that the person of the risen Jesus was as real and as material as those to whom he appeared. On this view tape recorders and video cameras would both have recorded them. If people did not always recognize him straightway, that was because they were not expecting to meet him. The fact that the risen Jesus could appear and disappear at will, and could pass through closed doors, and eat broiled fish, is irrelevant, the protagonists of this view would maintain. They would say that we simply do not know what is and what is not possible in the world of psychic phenomena. Very probably they would add that Jesus is utterly unique inasmuch as he had a divine nature, and what is impossible for ordinary people was possible for him. In any case these appearances might have been directly miraculous, inasmuch as God brought them into being, for with God nothing is impossible.

There is no way of proving or disproving such an argument. It is certainly never possible to disprove a miracle on the grounds that such a case is inadmissible. But there are drawbacks. We have no way, on this premise, of relating these appearances of Jesus to ordinary life, and for this reason to many people they will sound very implausible. Some wise words of Dr Austen Farrer are worth recalling:

The signs or evidences of Christ's Resurrection cannot be separable from the fact of it; they are the touches made by that fact on the disciples' minds and senses, or else on their physical environment. How can such touches fail to carry something of the uniqueness belonging to the reality which imprints them? But then, to take the other side of the argument, they cannot be simply unique, either; for what is Christ's would-be disciple then to make of them, or on what warrant to believe them? Evidently we must compromise. The facts (assuming them to be forthcoming) which can act as sufficient signs or evidences cannot be identical with any other facts, but neither can they be incomparable with all other facts whatsoever: they must bear an analogy to something.[35]

(2) Subjective Hallucinations

A very different kind of explanation is possible. Jesus' disciples may indeed have experienced appearances of the risen Jesus, but that these were delusions or subjective hallucinations. They could have resulted in experiences of the risen Jesus which were for the people concerned real experiences, but which at the same time were purely subjective, and originated in their own brains. Subjective hallucinations can be pathological, caused by drugs or alcohol, or they may be self-generated psychologically by people of unstable personality or who are in a high state of emotional expectancy or emotional stress. There is, of course, no suggestion in the gospels that the disciples were taking hallucinogenic drugs! (For that we have to turn to the fantasies of the late John Allegro and his 'sacred mushrooms'.) As for the suggestion that the disciples after the Crucifixion were in a highly emotional state of expectancy or stress, they were, on the contrary, as we have already noted, in a depressed and disillusioned state. This is the very opposite psychological frame of mind to that which gives rise to hallucinations.

It is sometimes said that all subjective hallucinations are personal to the person who suffers them, and that they cannot be shared with others. Since they are caused by factors within the brain, whether this be drugs or psychological states, they are private to the person concerned. It is true that subjective hallucinations are usually of this kind, but well attested examples of collective subjective hallucinations do exist, and this can perhaps best be explained by telepathic communication among those who are present. A good example of this is the collective hallucination which took hold of an expectant crowd at Fatima so that they saw the sun rushing towards the earth. Since the disciples of Jesus were not unduly stressed or expectant, the Resurrection appearances which are recorded in the New Testament do not meet this criterion, with two possible exceptions: the five hundred brethren of whom Paul wrote, who could conceivably have been in a high state of emotional expectation (because we know nothing about the circumstances of this appearance), and Paul at the time of his conversion (who certainly was under some stress at the time). And so, with these possible exceptions, subjective hallucination seems an improbable explanation of the Resurrection appearances.

(3) Veridical Hallucinations

There is another type of explanation, which involves what is known as 'veridical hallucination'.[36] While this cannot provide us with a complete explanation, it could give us a pointer towards it. It is not unknown for a person who is in some relationship to another person to see that person, or to hear words spoken by that person, either at the moment of death or shortly after death. There are many authenticated records of this held by the Society for Psychic Research. The phrase 'veridical hallucination' is not very satisfactory. 'Hallucination' is used because such experiences would not be recorded by camera or tape recorder; but 'veridical' indicates that the hallucination is observed in connection with a real event, which could afterwards be verified, although the percipient did not know this at the time when the hallucination occurred. There is often a coincidence of time – the phantasm may occur at the precise time of death. Such veridical hallucinations do not need any special conditions, such as a psychological condition of strain or expectancy on the part of the percipient. The experience is often comparatively short, but in some cases (as in the famous case of Miss Moberly's and Miss Jourdain's experiences at Versailles) it may last for some considerable time. In 80 per cent of the recorded cases, there is a link between those who experienced it and those whom they experienced. In contrast to subjective hallucinations, the person is experienced in vivid detail. The sense of touch as well as sight can be affected, although it is rare that the percipient is actually permitted to touch the person concerned. Although there are no instances of collective veridical hallucinations, we know that, in the subjective type, hallucination is likely to spread if the percipient is in company with others, and the same could be the case with 'veridical hallucination'.

There are here some clear parallels – as well as differences – with the Resurrection appearances. The disciples of course were well aware that Jesus was dead (herein lies the main difference) but there was present an element of extreme surprise: the last thing that they expected was to meet with Jesus. Another difference is that it cannot be said that the Resurrection appearances are veridical in the sense that they contain any verifiable information. Against these differences must be put some remarkable similarities. In the first place, as with 'veridical hallucinations', Jesus appeared after he was dead. Again, the person of Jesus was perceived in great detail. There are times, none the less, when he was not immediately recognized, but that too can be paralleled in 'veridical hallucinations' and its explanation may lie in the fact that the percipients never expected to see him. Furthermore, Jesus appeared 'not to the whole people, but to witnesses whom God had chosen in advance – to us, who ate and drank with him after he rose from the dead'; that is to say, to those with whom he had links. The people to whom he appeared were not emotionally disturbed, nor under great stress, nor in a state of expectancy. He appeared suddenly, and disappeared suddenly, as in cases of veridical hallucination. We are told that the women by the tomb clasped his feet, but this may have been a touch added to indicate their worship of him. He did not allow Mary Magdalene to touch him, and Thomas, although challenged, did not feel the need to do so. Touching a phantasm, while not unknown in cases of veridical hallucination, is very rare.

We can only surmise how veridical hallucinations can take place. We must presume that the person who is perceived, although dead yet in some way is still alive and through telepathy he communicates with the percipient so that he sees and hears (and may even touch) the person whom he perceives to be communicating with him. Of course we do not know the form in which the person concerned is alive after he has died. A mere discarnate mind would seem to be less than a person, passive and unable to relate to others. We must presume that such a person has some kind of spiritual, immaterial body, although we can have no idea of its real nature. The appearance of this person (whom we may call a phantasm), although he is actually seen and heard (and touched) by the percipient, is a hallucination in the sense that it would not be recorded by a camera or a tape recorder.

The resemblances between this kind of appearance and the Resurrection appearances of Jesus are sufficiently close for veridical hallucination to be considered as a pointer towards their explanation. (This, incidentally, would explain why, in his Resurrection stories, Jesus always appeared fully clothed.) Despite the fact that they are hallucinatory, they do in fact affirm the substantial reality of Jesus behind the Resurrection appearances. This would have been his mode of communicating with his disciples after his death, whereby he clothed his invisible and inaudible presence embodied in his new glorious body, with their earthly categories of physical perception. It was Jesus' means of communication with his disciples, which was more than merely telepathic, and by which he filled them with joy and assured them of his living presence, as he gave them orders and told them not to be afraid.

This could only be a pointer towards understanding the nature of the Resurrection appearances. Veridical hallucinations by themselves are quite inadequate to explain them. In the first place, the number of Jesus' Resurrection appearances is quite untypical of veridical hallucinations, which are rare and infrequent. In the second place, we cannot find in veridical hallucination an explanation of the continuing reversal of the disciples' attitudes which these appearances brought about, with their awakened sense of mission and purpose, their powerful and effective preaching of the Gospel and their buoyant fellowship and fearless outspokenness. In the records of psychic research we do not find this kind of effect resulting from other people's experiences of veridical hallucination. Finally, for those who believe that Jesus was God incarnate, the appearances of ordinary men and women who have died can only be a pointer towards appearances of him in whom Christians believe human nature and divine nature were united.

We have now considered various possible explanations of the Resurrection appearances of Jesus. Either they developed as ways of embodying truths about Jesus, or they were real experiences. If the latter, either they were appearances of the risen Lord which were objectively real, in the sense that they could in principle have been recorded on tape and formed the subject of a video, or they were subjective, in the sense that the recording and video tapes would have remained blank. If the latter, they could either have been 'subjective hallucinations' that is to say, hallucinations which had their origin solely within the brains and minds of their recipients, or they might have been something like veridical hallucinations and constituted a genuine mode of communication between the risen Jesus and his disciples without having in themselves a physical reality.

The Empty Tomb

Our view about the empty tomb will partly be determined by the explanation which we think is most plausible for Jesus' Resurrection appearances. What are the possible explanations that can be given of the empty tomb? We have already had occasion to notice some naturalistic explanations, when examining earlier in this book the gospel accounts of Jesus' death and of the discovery of the empty tomb; and we have regarded them as unlikely to provide the solution to the problem. It may be useful to tabulate this kind of explanation:

(1) The Swoon Theory

The theory that Jesus fainted on the Cross, later revived and then escaped from the tomb, may be quickly dismissed. People who suffer the cruel fate of crucifixion do not revive sufficiently to escape after they have been buried. Jesus in any case was certified before Pilate as dead. He could not have moved the stone from the inside. There is no hint in any reputable document from antiquity that Jesus was resuscitated, and resumed a normal life.

(2) Theft of the Body by the Jews

This theory may also be summarily rejected. If the Jews had the body they would have produced it when it was claimed that he had risen from the dead, even if they had stolen it in order to bury it in the plot set aside for those condemned to death. If they had stolen the body, they would surely not have left the stone rolled away from the tomb.

(3) Theft of the Body by the Disciples

This theory also may be rejected summarily. If the disciples had stolen the body they would have reverenced it like that of a martyr. In fact that never happened to the place of Jesus' burial until much later when pilgrimages to the Holy Sepulchre began. Why would the disciples have left the stone rolled away from the tomb? The disciples would surely not have stolen the body in order to pretend that Jesus had risen from the dead. We cannot in that way account for their continuing change of mood from dejection to confidence and faith, nor is this consonant with the evident authenticity of their faith and confidence in God.

(4) Mistaken Sepulchre

The suggestion has been made that the women coming early in the morning before it was properly light went to the wrong tomb, and found it empty, and that Jesus' body remained securely buried where it had been placed on Friday evening. This theory too may be confidently dismissed. It does not account for the Resurrection stories. The women were not the only visitors to the tomb, nor was it visited only at that very early hour of the day;

nor would the women, if they had watched the burial on Friday night, have been likely to make such an error.

There remain only a fifth and a sixth possibility. Either the story of the empty tomb is a story that grew up as a kind of *haggadah* on the event of the Resurrection, or it represents what actually was found to be the case.

(5) Development of a Myth?

Professor Lampe has explained how in his view, the myth of the empty tomb (as he understood it) came into being:

> It remains to ask why, if the empty tomb was not an original or essential part of the Easter message, it came to take so prominent a place in the story. The answer is that this was very natural. Once Christians began to reflect on the original proclamation that God raised Jesus and that he was seen alive by many witnesses, they would naturally picture the event of his raising in terms of an empty tomb. Particularly would this be true of men who were accustomed to the beliefs of Pharisaic Judaism about future life; though the tendency would not be entirely confined to them. But the natural inclination to view it in this way would be greatly stimulated by thinking on the scriptures. When Christians searched the Old Testament for texts bearing on the Resurrection they would be struck by Psalm 16:10: 'Thou wilt not abandon my soul to Hades, nor let thy loyal servant see corruption.' This prophecy was a powerful weapon in the armoury of Christian apologetics. It is cited in Acts 2:27 and Acts 13:35. It would immediately suggest that the raising of Jesus ought to be conceived in terms of a physical Resurrection of the body. From that point the story would inevitably come to be built up, as we can see it growing in the gospels.[37]

I have quoted my old tutor at length out of *pietas*; but there are difficulties in accepting the reasoning which this passage contains. Firstly, in our examination of Paul's thinking, we have left it as an open question whether he meant his words to be understood as assuming that there had been a physical Resurrection of Jesus:

on the whole it seems probable (although not certain) that he did. Secondly, if it was natural in the time of Jesus 'to picture the event of his raising in terms of an empty tomb', and if God wished to make it known that Jesus had been raised, it seems appropriate that he would have caused the tomb to be empty, and to be seen to be empty. Thirdly, we have already considered the citations of Psalm 16:10 and the difficulties involved in supposing that it gave rise, or helped to give rise, to a story of the empty tomb. In any case we have to account for the growth of a legend during the lifetime of those who would have known that it was false. St John's gospel, as we have already noted, contains some very primitive tradition and may even be by the hand of John the Apostle himself. St Mark's gospel was published if not before, then soon after the death of Peter. There must have been many people younger than he who knew the truth of the matter. How could the author of Mark (and of the other gospels) have made so much of the empty tomb if it was only a story 'we can see growing in the gospels'?

Are the differences in the four gospels about the finding of the empty tomb the kind of differences which are to be expected when different sources and traditions are used by the various evangelists in an age which did not share our contemporary passion for 'scientific history'? Each must answer that question according to his personal judgement; but it may be useful to list the differences between the various accounts. They concern (i) the time when the women appeared. All the gospels agree that it was about the time of dawn, but there is some divergence whether it was before, at or shortly after dawn. (ii) The earthquake and the guard, alone recorded by St Matthew are suspect for reasons already given. (iii) The reason why the women came to the tomb; to anoint Jesus' body (Mark and Matthew) or just to be there (Luke and John). (iv) The exact identity of the women who found the stone rolled away; Mary Magdalene, Mary of Joseph, and Salome (Mark), Mary Magdalene and the other Mary (Matthew), the women (Luke), Mary Magdalene alone (John). Mary at least seems common to them all. (v) The mysterious beings they met; a young man clad in white (Mark), the angel (Matthew), two men in gleaming apparel (Luke), two angels (John). (vi) The words spoken by these beings, the theological significance of which may sufficiently explain the differences in the synoptic gospels. In St John's gospel it is not asserted, as in the other gospels, that Jesus has risen, but Mary Magdalene is asked why she is weeping. The fact that Jesus appeared to her immediately after she had spoken to the angel makes it unnecessary for him to assert that Jesus had risen. (vii) The visit of Peter and the beloved disciple, told only in St John's gospel.

(6) The Physical Resurrection of Jesus

There is one factor that is common to all of the four accounts of the empty tomb, and this is that Mary Magdalene went to the tomb and found it empty, and had a vision there which assured her that Jesus had risen from the dead. But this, together with the accounts of the Resurrection stories, is quite insufficient to establish the fact of the empty tomb and the disappearance of Jesus' corpse. For this to be made credible we need to give a connected account of what may have happened which takes into account the gospel evidence.

Such a reconstruction may certainly be attempted. The women did not return to the tomb in order to anoint the body, for they could not have rolled away the stone by themselves, and there was no one else there before dawn to help them. They came to take another look at the tomb from which they had had to beat a hasty retreat on Friday evening because of the onset of the Sabbath. They knew that there had not been time to wash the body before it was laid out, and this would have left them uneasy. How had the matter been left? They were not sure, and they decided to find out before anyone else was about. They had had no time to grieve at the tomb, and they badly needed to do this on their own. So they set out early, just before dawn. The Fourth Evangelist seems to have had access to a separate and probably reliable source for the events of Holy Week and Sunday morning. Mary Magdalene may have set out with some other women to the tomb; they may have found it empty and run away; Mary may have gone to tell Peter and the other disciples; two came and found the tomb empty, and the stone rolled away; Mary returned with them, and she was left alone there, weeping by the empty tomb; and Jesus, whom she at first mistook for the gardener, appeared to her there. Mary Magdalene at first seemed to think that the gardener had stolen the body probably on behalf of the Jews ('Tell me where you have laid him and I will take him away'). As for the angel (or young man in white), it is impossible for us now to know exactly what was seen or heard. Maybe, in an age which believed in angels, this was the way in which they expressed, and indeed experienced, their conviction that Jesus was risen.

A satisfactory explanation about what happened must be distinguished from an explanation why it happened. We have already noted that the rolling away of the stone as an event must be distinguished from the Resurrection itself. Its object would have been to make known that the tomb was empty. Why was it necessary for the body to disappear? Here we are in the realm of mystery. If the theory of 'veridical hallucination' does shed light on the Resurrection appearances of Jesus, then we cannot say that it was *necessary* for the body to disappear in order for the risen Jesus to cause the disciples to experience his appearances in the way that they did. The physical bodies of other people experienced in veridical hallucinations have not disappeared.

We are not privy to the mind of God in the matter of Jesus' Resurrection. It could be that if there was a physical Resurrection, his body dematerialized in order to make public the fact that God had indeed raised Jesus from the dead, and that the stone was rolled back for the same reason. On the other hand, an alternative explanation might be that, since his Resurrection appearances were more frequent and (in some cases) longer and more detailed (with words spoken and commands given) than is the case with other veridical hallucinations, dematerialization was needed. But, if Jesus' body did disappear, it seems likely to have been connected with the mystery of his divine nature. There are those who say that his bones remain lying in Palestine beneath the rubble of centuries. But would this be appropriate in the unique case of him in whose person were united both human and divine natures? If his body disappeared, this could well be the explanation.

In this study an attempt has been made to put before the reader the relevant evidence, and the various explanations that have been given both to the Virginal Conception of Jesus and to the empty tomb. The reader has been confronted with a series of choices, as though he had to make them for himself. While at the end of the day he has to decide for himself, he may be also a member of the Christian Church. We must next consider how his views would be shaped by the Church of which he may be a loyal and faithful member.

Chapter 14

The Faith of the Church

The Creeds

If we are to examine the beliefs of the Church down the ages about the Virginal Conception of Jesus and his physical Resurrection and the claims that these beliefs make on members of the Church, we need to look at its foundation documents. Right back in the very early days of the primitive Church there emerged short terse summaries of the Christian faith for general use. This tendency to credal formulae can even be seen within the New Testament itself. By AD 150 the Old Roman Creed was already in use, the earliest creed known to us. It is basically the same as what we know today as 'The Apostles' Creed'. Other forms of creed later evolved, to counter false teaching and to meet the needs of the time. The creeds have always been treated with great respect throughout Christendom. No other statements of the Christian faith have greater authority among all the Churches down the centuries. We need therefore to consider carefully what is included (and what is not included) in the creeds on the two subjects into which we are enquiring.

There is a clause on Virginal Conception right back in the Old Roman Creed. It was included in subsequent creeds, and forms part of the catholic creeds of Christendom. It could therefore be said to be a foundation Christian belief, and many would say that it should be accepted on that authority by all Christians. If there is any doubt about the evidence concerning the Virginal Conception of Jesus, the fact that it has always been included in these credal formulations ought to settle the matter. It has always been part of the belief of Christendom.

This argument appears at first sight to be very strong. But there are some further important considerations which need to be examined and which point in a rather different direction.

All creeds include a clause about Christ's Ascension into the heavens. No doubt originally this was interpreted literally. Nowadays most people interpret the clause symbolically to describe Jesus' ascendency over all things. Although the symbolism of height may be needed to indicate transcendence, we now know that the planet is spinning on its axis, and circling the Sun, and that the whole Milky Way is revolving. We know that there can be no 'above' and 'below' in any absolute sense, except for 'flat earthers'. In any case, heaven is not to be understood as a locality in any physical sense, certainly not to be located 'above the bright blue sky'. It is no more necessary to believe that Jesus literally went up into the heavens than it is to hold that he is literally seated at the right hand of God. If the latter indicates his authority, the former declares his ascendency. A literal view of the Ascension was acceptable in the first century AD, but our more recent knowledge of the 'heavenly bodies' (the word is still in use) makes it necessary to re-interpret it. This does not mean that the phrase 'ascended into heaven' ought to be deleted from the Creed. Far from it. The phrase symbolizes the ascendency of Christ over all things, and as such it is a most important clause. It is simply that we interpret it symbolically and not literally. It can be argued that we should deal with the Virginal Conception in the same way. If the Ascension can be interpreted in this way to describe Jesus' departure from the world, cannot the Virginal Conception also be interpreted symbolically to describe his coming into the world? It is important that the clause should be retained, the proponents of this view would say, because it makes clear Christ's divine origin, and the divine initiative which resulted in the Incarnation.

Some Christians believe literally the statement in the creeds that Jesus 'will come again to judge both the quick and the dead'; but here again many take this as a symbol of the truth that God will be victorious, and his victory will be openly acknowledged and his purposes for his world will finally prevail. For some their knowledge of the heavenly bodies makes literal acceptance of the phrase very difficult. As the sun nears the end of its life it will swell into a 'red giant', making the earth too hot for human habitation, or indeed to support any form of life at all. That will be the end of the life of man, according to our present understanding, unless before that time he has managed to transfer his habitat to somewhere else in the galaxy. It may be that some irruption from elsewhere in the galaxy will bring life to an end before that, or perhaps man will bring this on himself through ecological catastrophe. We cannot predict the future of our planet exactly. But in New Testament times there was an entirely different vista of the future, with which the Second Coming of Christ was entirely compatible, and within which the belief developed. While we tend to think today in terms of an evolving universe, the Jews tended to think in terms of different epochs and a final denouement. However a warning against too facile a re-interpretation of this doctrine is given by those who believe in a literal Second Coming. They are fearful lest the Church falls victim to contemporary fashions and secular ways of thinking. God is all powerful, and the return of his Son to earth has been promised, and if this goes against current expectations, so much the worse for them. It is, however, important to note that both those who interpret the Second Coming literally and those who give it a symbolic meaning insist on the retention of the phrase, because eschatology (the doctrine of the last things) forms an important aspect of the Christian Gospel.

Some claim that the Virginal Conception may be interpreted symbolically in the same kind of way as the Ascension and the Second Coming. Others believe that the creeds should be accepted literally as they stand. It is not the clauses of the creeds that are disputed, nor their vital importance for Christian teaching, but simply whether they must be literally interpreted or may be interpreted symbolically. What at first sight appeared a cut and dried matter turns out on inspection to be much more complex!

When we turn from the Virginal Conception to the empty tomb, we find that the Old Roman Creed mentions the 'resurrection of the flesh' (*resurrectio carnis*). But in the Creed this refers not to the Resurrection of Jesus but to the Resurrection of all believers at the Last Day. However the very use of the phrase betrays a certain departure from the Pauline teaching that 'flesh and blood cannot enter the Kingdom of God'. (The so-called Athanasian Creed contains a reference to all men 'rising with their bodies' at the coming of Christ; but this is a much later document, neither properly a creed nor composed by Athanasius!) Early Western creeds contained a phrase about Jesus, after his death, descending to the place of departed spirits (*descendit ad inferos*), and this is included in our present 'Apostles' Creed'. It refers to the passage in 1 Peter 3:19 which affirms that Jesus after his death went and preached 'to the imprisoned spirits': it was probably included in the Creed to emphasize that Jesus really did die. But there is no mention of an empty tomb in any creed. None the less all the creeds emphasized that Jesus was 'dead and buried', and we have already noted that the emphasis on the burial of Jesus in connection with his Resurrection suggests (but does not prove) that it was a physical Resurrection. Although the early compilers of the Creed took for granted that his tomb was empty and that Jesus rose physically from the dead, there is no explicit mention of this in any creed, and a person who is agnostic about this (or even who denies it) cannot strictly be accused of not endorsing the Christian creeds.

For some people the fact that both the Virginal Conception and the empty tomb are found in Scripture, and that the empty tomb is found in Scripture and implied in the Creeds, is sufficient spiritual authority for their literal acceptance. Others believe that it is compatible with their interpretation as symbolic truths.

The Faith of the Church of England

So far we have considered only the spiritual authority of the Church of God as a divinely ordained organism. But the Church also consists of human institutions and institutions have their own rules and regulations. We need to consider the authority of these human ecclesial bodies. In a work of this kind we cannot consider all the rulings of all the Churches on the Virginal Conception and the physical Resurrection of Jesus. We shall therefore confine our attention to the only Church well known to the author, that to which he belongs, the Church of England.

(1) The Thirty-nine Articles of Religion

The Thirty-nine Articles of Religion have always been regarded as a key document of the Church of England. The Articles nowhere require belief in the inerrancy of Scripture. Article VI merely asserts that it contains all things necessary for salvation. Article II affirms that 'the Son . . . took Man's nature in the womb of the blessed Virgin, of her substance'. This assumes the traditional view that Mary supplied the humanity of Jesus, when the Incarnation took place. Article IV asserts that 'Christ did truly rise again from the dead, and took again his body, with flesh, bones and all things pertaining to the perfection of man's nature . . .' This article was written against the Anabaptist position which seemed to sit light to Christ's humanity, and which was felt to deny its reality after the Resurrection. As the Article reads, it seems to imply that the eternal Son, the second person of the Blessed Trinity, was in some way permanently changed by the Incarnation through the addition of Christ's full humanity. But the thrust of the Article has little bearing on the question of the empty tomb. No doubt this is assumed in the formularies of the Church of England, but it is not explicitly mentioned in them.

However the authority of the Thirty-nine Aarticles is no longer so great as it used to be. Until the law was changed, every clergyman had to subscribe to all the Articles as 'agreeable to the Word of God'. But recently the terms of subscription have been altered. Now the Declaration of Assent speaks of 'the faith uniquely revealed in the catholic creeds, which faith the Church is called upon to proclaim afresh in each generation. Led by the Holy Spirit it has borne witness to Christian truth in its historical formularies, the Thirty-nine Articles of Religion, the Book of

Common Prayer and the Ordering of Bishops, Priests and Deacons. A clergyman is asked: 'In the declaration you are about to make, will you affirm your loyalty to this inheritance of faith as your inspiration and guidance under God in bringing the grace and truth of God to this generation and making him known to those in your care?' No specific loyalty is required to the literal acceptance of all the Articles. And so in this respect acceptance of the Virginal Conception and the empty tomb cannot be said to be required by the law of the land in the Declaration of Assent.

(2) Doctrine in the Church of England

The Virginal Conception of Jesus and of his physical Resurrection were the subject of national controversy at the nomination of Dr Hensley Henson, Dean of Durham, to the see of Hereford in 1929. Dr Henson had made statements about the Virginal Conception and the physical Resurrection of Christ not dissimilar in content (although very different in style) from those made by Dr David Jenkins on his nomination to the see of Durham. In a memorandum written by Dr Davidson, then Archbishop of Canterbury, and published by his biographer, Davidson records Dr Henson's viewpoint:

> He in no sense denies the truth of that narrative as traditionally interpreted, or of the narrative of the Resurrection. But with regard to the details, he adopts a position of what he calls Christian Agnosticism considering it to be true to say that the progress of human knowledge forces us to state historic facts in different ways in different epochs.[38]

The archbishop persuaded Dr Henson to write him a formal letter which enabled him to go ahead and consecrate him as a bishop, and which silenced controversy for the time being. (A formal letter of this kind might well also have defused the dispute about the controversy of Dr Jenkins as Bishop of Durham.) Yet unease about the matter persisted, not without cause; and Dr Charles Gore, the Bishop of Oxford, who had originally led the campaign against Dr Henson, persuaded the archbishop to set up in 1929 a Commission to examine doctrine in the Church of England. This body took a long time to do its work, and its report was not published until 1938. It was a prestigious body, and Dr William Temple, the future Archbishop of Canterbury, had become its chairman. Its report was entitled 'Doctrine in the Church of England' since the commission had no authority to determine what actually is the doctrine of the Church of England.

In an appended note to their Report, the Commission stated that they regarded the symbolic interpretation of certain phrases in the creeds as justified, and considered that 'it is far better for us to learn to use them with an interpretation suited to our needs than to discard them for others more obviously expressive of present habits of thought.' The note continued:

> In some cases the use of traditional phrases is regarded as dishonest. This charge could only be sustained if the traditional phrase is being used in a sense wholly different from that originally conveyed by it. That it should be used to represent a meaning partly identical with, and partly different from, that which in the mind of those who first employed it is simply what happens to some extent to all language as the context of thought is altered from one generation to another. The reason for the continued use of such phrases is that there is a core meaning of identical meaning.[39]

This general statement needs to be applied to the particular instance of the Virginal Conception. The Report went on to point out that this must not be seen in isolation from the totality of beliefs about the person and work of Christ. It agreed that belief in the Virginal Conception as a historical fact cannot be independent of the historical evidence, although it had to confess that, in this case, the historical evidence cannot be anything other than inconclusive. The Report commented on its importance for doctrine as follows:

> It is a safeguard of the Christian conviction that in the birth of Jesus we have, not simply the birth of a new individual of the human species, but the advent of One who 'for us men and for our salvation came down from heaven'. It is congruous with

the belief that in the person of Christ mankind made a fresh beginning. It coheres with the supernatural element in the life of Christ, indicating a unique inauguration of that unique life. It gives expression to the idea of the response of the human race to God's purpose through the obedience and faith of the Blessed Virgin Mary.[40]

The Report then went to on set out two different views side by side. The first was the traditional view that belief in the Word made flesh is integrally bound up with belief in the Virginal Conception, and that this will be increasingly recognized. The second view was set out as follows:

There are however some among us who hold that a full belief in the historical Incarnation is more consistent with the supposition that our Lord's birth took place under the normal conditions of human generation. In their minds the notion of a Virgin Birth tends to mar the completeness of the belief that in the Incarnation God revealed himself at every point in and through human nature.[41]

Both these views were held among members of the Commission, although the traditional view, which Archbishop Temple himself held (although earlier difficulties about it had led to delays in his own ordination) predominated among its members.

The Commission also dealt in its report with the question of the empty tomb. With reference to the Resurrection we find the following:

When we attempt to go beyond the *kerygma*, and ask 'What was it that actually happened?' a variety of answers is possible. Belief that the Lord was risen – the acceptance of the *kerygma* itself – is compatible both with a realisation that we cannot expect to reach clear or full knowledge in detail, and also with a variety of critical views. If a general principle is to be laid down, we may say that the Christian faith is compatible with all such critical reconstructions of the events underlying the narratives as would not have the effect, if accepted, of invalidating the apostolic testimony to Jesus as the Lord who rose from the dead. To speak more positively, we are of the opinion that it ought to be affirmed that Jesus was veritably alive and victorious; that He showed Himself, alive from the dead, to the disciples; and that the fact of His rising, however explained (and it involves probably an element beyond our explaining), is to be understood to have been an event as real and concrete as the crucifixion itself (which it reversed) and an act of God, wholly unique in human history. The symbol of this fact in the gospels is the story of the empty tomb. More than one explanation of this has been suggested; but the majority of the Commission are agreed in holding the traditional explanation – viz., that the tomb was empty because the Lord had risen.[42]

Once again the traditional view predominated among members of the Commission but loyal members of the Church of England (including members of the Commission) held a different interpretation while still affirming the reality of the risen Lord.

It so happens that shortly after the Report was published, the second Great War broke out, and there was no discussion of it, and so it has never been officially endorsed. There was understandably considerable opposition to it at the time among the traditionally minded clergy, but it was regarded as having considerable authority by reason of the eminence of its members. The Convocation of York, however, did discuss it, and passed a resolution which Archbishop Runcie quoted when he was speaking about the controversial remarks of Bishop Jenkins:

The history of the Church supplies much evidence of the unwisdom in any attempt to limit interpretation by authoritative declaration: we are convinced that the wisest course is not to prescribe the interpretation in addition to the standard itself.

(3) The Nature of Christian Belief
The two clauses referring to the Virginal Conception and the empty tomb in the Statement of the House of Bishops, made in 1986, were cited in the Introduction, and they are repeated again

here for convenience. In connection with the Virginal Conception the bishops said:

> As regards the Virginal Conception of our Lord, we acknowledge and uphold belief in this as expressing the faith of the Church of England, and as affirming that in Christ God has taken the initiative for our salvation by uniting with himself our human nature, so bringing to birth a new humanity.

In their Exposition of the Statement, the bishops commented:

> The central miracle, the heart of the Christian understanding of God, is the Incarnation itself. It is the faith of us all that this is truly expressed in the affirmation of the Christian creeds that in Jesus, fully God and fully human, the Second Person of the Blessed Trinity is incarnate. The divergence between scholars on the relation of the Virginal Conception of our Lord to this great mystery, and on the question whether or not that Conception is to be regarded as historical fact as well as imagery symbolic of divine truth, have been indicated and they are reflected in the convictions of members of this House.

So far as the empty tomb is concerned the bishops included this in their Statement:

> As regards belief that Christ's tomb was empty on the first Easter Day, we acknowledge and uphold this as expressing the faith of the Church of England, and as affirming that in the resurrection life the material order is redeemed, and the fulness of human nature, bodily, mental and spiritual, is glorified for eternity.

In the Exposition of the Statement the bishops explained further their position:

> This faith in the Resurrection is the faith of every member of this House. On the question whether, as a result of this divine act, Christ's tomb that first Easter Day was empty we recognise that scholarship can offer no conclusive demonstration; and the divergent views to be found among scholars of standing are

reflected in the thinking of individual Bishops. But all of us accept first, that belief that the tomb was empty can be held with full intellectual integrity; secondly, that this is the understanding of the witness of Scripture which is generally received in the universal Church; and thirdly, that this House acknowledges and upholds this belief as expressing the faith of the Church of England and of its historic teaching . . .[43]

This Report, while received by General Synod, was not specifically endorsed by that body; but it has the authority that is proper to the House of Bishops in an episcopal Church.

Summary

We have now concluded our examination of the two subjects of the Virginal Conception of Jesus and of the empty tomb. The evidence of the gospels and the rest of the New Testament has been set out in a way which is intended to be fair and unbiased; and the same applies to considerations of their doctrinal implications, as well as to relevant modern scientific knowledge in so far as this applies. We have also considered the spiritual authority of the Christian Church in its conservation of the truth of the Christian Gospel, and also the particular requirements of the Church of England in these matters. The reader should now be in a better position to make up his or her own mind on these matters.

But they are very complex. The two questions with which this book started: 'Was Jesus the child of a virgin?' and 'Was he raised physically from the dead?' are so simple. But to answer a historical question about events which took place nearly two thousand years ago, for which the evidence may be disputed, is the very reverse of simple. A large number of disciplines are involved, which include a knowledge of languages and the relevant literature, the dating of the New Testament books which comprise the primary evidence, the probable dates when those books were written, the principles of textual criticism, knowledge about the form and the theology as well as the contents of those books, and the comparative study of the differences to be found in the gospels and the relationships between them. In addition to this there must be some knowledge about the history of the period, from secular as well as from religious sources, and also some knowledge about scientific hypotheses which might be thought to explain some of the evidence. It will be noted too how Christian doctrine is interrelated. In order to investigate the Virginal Conception and the empty tomb, we have had not only to consider the doctrine of the Incarnation and of Resurrection, but also the Christian doctrines of creation, original sin, providence and grace, and the relationship of the conception of Jesus to his baptism and Resurrection, and we have had to relate the doctrine of the Incarnation to the doctrines of the Atonement, Ascension, and Second Coming. We have also had to consider the 'hierarchy of truth' in Christian doctrine.

It seems ridiculous to invite the average layman or laywoman to make up their minds about these two questions without even a working knowledge of these different disciplines. Perhaps they will decide simply to opt for the traditional solution – yes, Jesus was born of a virgin, and yes, he did rise from the dead, simply on grounds of the spiritual authority of Scripture and/or the Church. If so, their troubles are at an end, and in a sense such people have perhaps been wasting their time reading this book. But there are others who may not feel able to accept the historicity of the facts under discussion simply on the authority of the Scriptures (for they need interpreting) or that of the Church to which they belong (which may not be explicit on the need for a literal rather than symbolic interpretation). This may well be the case if they are aware of people whose judgement they admire within their Church who are not able to accept the traditional answers to these questions.

What are such people to do? Presumably they need help from theologians who are trained in such disciplines. But they need to exercise some caution here. There are two sorts of theologians. One group is employed by the Church, either in seminaries, or in universities or religious foundations, or in religious Orders, not to mention the bishops and clergy. It is a fact of experience that most of such theologians tend to opt for the traditional answers of the Church. The second group is employed in the universities of this land, either in departments of theology or departments of religion. These departments have a special need for the regard of their colleagues in other departments of the university, for there is a tendency in these institutions, strange as it may seem, to regard theology as a soft option, and (among some critics) as an unsuitable subject for university study. It must be remembered that the universities of Britain are strongly imbued with the ethos of the Enlightenment, searching for rational answers to problems and tending to discount claims of the supernatural. Again, it is a fact of experience that university teaching officers in departments of theology are apt to opt for naturalistic answers to questions about the conception of Jesus and the nature of his Resurrection.

It must be borne in mind, however, that although these are important questions, they are not the most important questions which Christians have to ask, and it is perfectly possible for Christians in good standing to return different answers to them. The basic confessions of the Christian faith concern our commitment to God the Holy Trinity, and our belief that in Christ God became man for us and for our salvation, and that on the third day he rose again from the dead. These statements of faith can be made both by those who do and who do not accept the historicity of the Virginal Conception of Jesus and by those who do or who do not accept the physical Resurrection of Jesus from the dead. It would be far better for Christians on both sides to stop wasting the energies of the Church Militant through indulging in damaging internal warfare on these matters, and to concentrate instead on living the Gospel and sharing it with others and especially living in love and charity with their neighbours, with protagonists on both sides united in their commitment to the Incarnation of the Son of God and his Resurrection on the third day.

Epilogue

I have tried to write this book in such a way that the reader will be able to make up his or her own judgement about the 'Virgin Birth' and the empty tomb. But I do not want to use my attempted objectivity as a facade behind which to shelter, and it seems wrong to withhold my own views on the matter as though I had no convictions myself. In the last chapter of a detective story there is often a solution to the theft or murder which had never occurred to the reader because of the way in which the facts had been presented. Although there is a sense in which this enquiry has been an exercise in detection, there is no fiction involved, and no last minute surprise to be found in the last chapter. Indeed it may be that my conclusions seem inevitable from the way in which I have dealt with the presentation of the evidence, although I would like to think that it is the evidence itself which leads me to my conclusions.

I am agnostic about the Virginal Conception of Jesus, and I believe that the tomb was found empty after Jesus had been physically raised from the dead.

I must briefly give my reasons.

I am struck by the fact that nowhere in his recorded words does Jesus refer to the mode of his birth. I am puzzled too by the way in which his mother seems to join with the rest of the family in considering Jesus to be out of his mind near the start of his public ministry. I would have thought that, had there been a Virginal Conception, Mary would have told her son about his origins, and would not have been so disturbed by the way in which he was

conducting his public ministry. I am also struck by the great
differences between the birth and infancy narratives of St
Matthew's and St Luke's gospels, and by the theological motives
underlying these narratives and the ways in which they are told.
In particular the Matthean genealogy suggests that there was
some sexual irregularity in connection with Jesus' origins. The
possibility of Joseph divorcing his betrothed quietly without a
scandal seems too remote to be easily accepted, while the
historical details of the census seem inconsistent with the Lucan
account of Jesus' birth at Bethlehem, which casts doubt also on
the historicity of the Annunciation. If the Virginal Conception is
not based on historical facts, these stories are not so much
fabrications as *haggadah*, stories told to embody spiritual truths,
and as such perfectly acceptable.

Our knowledge of genetics makes it difficult to credit Jesus with
a full humanity if he had no human father, while the theological
truths underlying the Virginal Conception, e.g., Jesus' divine
nature, God's fresh initiative to save the human race, do not seem
to require a Virginal Conception; and Paul preached a powerful
gospel without referring to it, and indeed seems not to know
about it. If Jesus did have a human father, it was most likely to
have been Joseph, and he was likely to have been conceived
during the betrothal of Joseph and Mary. Such an occurrence
seems to me quite compatible with God's gracious action of
Incarnation.

On the other hand, I have lingering doubts that there may be
truth in the story of the Virginal Conception. Although I am
suspicious about the historicity of most of St Matthew's material
in his birth and infancy narratives, I am struck by the way in which
he almost takes for granted the fact of the Virginal Conception.
Also it is not easy to accept that all the birth and narrative stories
in St Luke's gospel are solely the result of his own imaginative
and creative skills. He may have been able to use sources which
were reliably based. In particular I find it hard to believe that the
story of Jesus' birth at Bethlehem was constructed from a few
obscure verses in Micah and a mistaken idea about a Roman
census; and similarly the story of the Visitation suggests not only

Old Testament echoes but also an actual event. And whatever we may know about our genetic make-up, I have no doubt that, if God wished to do so, he could have miraculously overridden the normalities of human reproduction. I cannot therefore deny the possibility of the Virginal Conception, but for the reasons given above, I cannot affirm it. I have to remain agnostic about its historicity, although of course I enthusiastically accept the doctrinal truths underlying it.

Turning to the physical Resurrection of Jesus, I have already given an account of how, on the basis of the gospels, the events may be reconstructed which led to the tomb being found empty with the stone rolled away; and I need not repeat them again here.

As a matter of fact I find the strongest argument against the empty tomb not the conflicting gospel accounts nor its intrinsic improbability but a doctrinal consideration. If Jesus was like to us in every way except without sin, why should he be raised to a new form of existence in a way different from that of other people? After all, we no longer expect the tombs to open at the Last Judgement, so that we shall then be raised to glory. My old tutor, Professor Geoffrey Lampe, for whom I have a deep respect, and whom I have quoted in an earlier chapter, felt this argument so deeply that it formed one of the main reasons why he did not believe in the empty tomb, although he had a profound conviction about Jesus being raised to life after his physical death, which movingly sustained him during his own terminal illness. He wrote of the hope and comfort given at countless funerals by the words of Baxter's well-known hymn:

> Christ leads me through no darker rooms
> Than he went through before;
> He that into God's kingdom comes
> Must enter by this door.

And he commented on this verse as follows: 'If the story of the empty tomb were true, Christ's door into God's kingdom would not be ours. We should be confronted by another door through which he has never entered: into a darker room which his presence has never lightened.'[44]

While appreciating the force of this argument, I am not convinced by it. We cannot lay down what is appropriate for God to do. If God wanted publicly to vindicate the death of his incarnate Son, who are we to say that it was inappropriate for him to raise Jesus by a mode which resulted in his tomb being found empty? God may have wished to point publicly to his vindication of his Son, and to mark out by a special act of power the action that he had taken for the salvation of the world. We cannot rule out the possibility of a miracle, just because miracles are very rare, or because they conflict with what used to be thought of as unalterable laws of nature. Incarnation, by its very nature, may involve the incarnate person being different in some respects from the rest of mankind, and so being raised to life in a different mode.

The miracle of the opening of the empty tomb, however, must not be confused with the miracle of Jesus being raised to life in such a way that the tomb was found to be empty. The two are connected but separate. It could be objected that it was entirely inappropriate for God to use an impersonal miracle of this type in connection with the Resurrection of Jesus, which was in no way dependent upon it; another of Bishop David Jenkins's 'laser beam miracles'. But without this no one would have known that this mighty act of God had actually taken place, other than through the testimony of those who saw him again. It was for our sakes and for our salvation that the Son of God 'came down from heaven', and was incarnate; and it was for our sakes and for our salvation that he conquered death, and was vindicated by his heavenly Father. If therefore salvation was to be offered to mankind in this way, it was necessary that mankind should be assured about what had occurred. The mere testimony of witnesses that they had seen the risen Jesus could be put down to subjective factors rather than to the objective reality of Jesus' Resurrection. If God put such a high value on the salvation of the human race, the empty tomb seems an appropriate corollary.

The empty tomb is affirmed in all four gospels, and I find no good reason to disbelieve it, or to suspend belief. The reality of Jesus' death and his subsequent burial in a hitherto unused rock tomb adjacent to where he was crucified is well attested. Similarly there is strong evidence, from three of the four gospels, of his appearances to his disciples on and for a period after the first Easter. The records of these appearances bear the hallmark of authentic experiences in which the disciples were convinced of the reality of the risen Jesus. The form of these stories in most cases points towards their authenticity. The differences between the four gospels about the appearances can be partly accounted for by their differing theologies about Jesus (particularly their differences of location), and partly by the different traditions which embody testimony about past events among witnesses whose memories differed. Paul's testimony, earlier than that of the written gospels, similarly attests the authenticity of the Resurrection appearances. Some pointer towards an understanding of these appearances may be gained by comparing them with records of 'veridical hallucinations'. The meaning of the appearances is unmistakable; Jesus' victory over the powers of evil by his death, his assurance to the disciples of his living presence, and his commands to tell them what to do.

As for the empty tomb, while it is improbable that the women came to the tomb to anoint the body, because there would have been no one to roll away the stone for them, it is very understandable that they decided to visit the tomb very early on Easter morning, since the funeral rites had not all been completed, and they had to rush away before the onset of the Sabbath, so they wanted a time of quiet to grieve there early in the morning. (I dismiss the possibility that they went to the wrong tomb, or that Jesus' body has been removed by human hands, or that Jesus revived in the tomb and escaped from the tomb.) As for the stone being rolled back, this could not have happened by chance, and as there is no indication that it happened by human hands, the presumption is that it must have been an act of God in order that it should be known that the tomb inside was empty. Despite differences of detail about the discovery of the empty tomb, it is well attested in all four gospels. One of the women, Mary Magdalene, rushed off to tell Peter and John that the stone had been taken away, and when they went in they found it empty.

I am particularly struck by John's testimony about the way the grave clothes were lying. While the physical Resurrection of Jesus is not mentioned elsewhere in the New Testament other than in the gospels, it seems to be implicit in the emphasis on Jesus' burial before his Resurrection, and also in the early traditions underlying speeches in the Acts of the Apostles.

This seems to me a very strong case in favour of the scriptural witness to the empty tomb and the physical Resurrection of Jesus. Of course we are in the realm of mystery, and in any case no certainty can be attained in reconstructing historical events which took place so long ago and for which there is not the wealth of evidence which would be available for contemporary events. For this reason, I respect those who, for good reasons, are agnostic about the empty tomb, or who even deny it, but who at the same time affirm the reality of Jesus' Resurrection and his victory over the powers of evil through his death. I disagree with them.

I am strong in my conviction that the tomb was empty when Jesus was raised from the dead. I am agnostic about the Virginal Conception, but I rejoice to join with others in the two ancient acclamations of the Church:

'Hail, Mary full of grace! Blessed art thou among women and blessed is the fruit of thy womb, Jesus!'

'Alleluiah, Christ is risen! He is risen indeed!'

Notes

1. *The Nature of Christian Belief*, Church House Publishing, 1986, pp. 1f.
2. Fr E. Yarnold, SJ 'Open Letter', *Newsletter of the Ecumenical Society of the Blessed Virgin Mary*, January 1987, in response to Hugh Montefiore, *So Far And Yet So Near*, SCM Press, 1986, pp. 63–75.
3. J. B. Lightfoot, *Saint Paul's Epistle to the Galatians*, Macmillan, 1987, pp. 252–91
4. L. Finkelstein, *The Pharisees*, Philadelphia, 1946, vol i, p. 46.
5. G. Vermes, *Jesus the Jew*, Collins, 1973, now SCM Press, pp. 218f.
6. R. R. Reuther, *Mary – The Feminine Face of the Church*, SCM Press, 1979, pp. 28f.
7. Hugh Montefiore, *Josephus and the New Testament*, Mowbray, 1962, pp. 8–16.
8. J. A. T. Robinson, *Redating the New Testament*, SCM Press, 1976, p. 107.
9. A. H. McNeile, *The Gospel According to St Matthew*, Macmillan, 1938, p. xxviii.
10. H. Conzelmann, *The Theology of St Luke*, ET, Faber, 1960; cf. also H. Flender, *St Luke Theologian of Redemptive History*, ET, SPCK, 1967.
11. R. Laurentin, *Structure et Theologie Luc 1–11*, Gabalda, Paris, pp. 64–90.
12. Hugh Montefiore, *A Commentary on the Epistle to the Hebrews*, Black, 1964, pp. 12ff.

13. A. v. Harnack, 'Zu Lc 1.34, 35', *Zeitschrift für die Neutestament-liche Wissenschaft*, vol. ii (1901), p. 53.

14. V. Taylor, *The Historical Evidence for the Virgin Birth*, London, 1920.

15. J. Brierley, *The Thinking Machine*, Heinemann, 1973, p. 12.

16. M. Wiles, *God's Action in the World*, SCM Press, 1986, pp. 92ff.

17. P. Brown, *The Body and Society*, Faber, 1990, p. 352.

18. P. Brown, *op. cit.*, p. 407.

19. Cf. U. Ranke-Heinemann, *Eunuchs for Society*, ET, Deutsch, 1990, p. 118f., 310f.

20. Marina Warner, *Alone Of All Her Sex*, Weidenfeld, 1976.

21. *The Nature of Christian Belief*, p. 32.

22. D. Jenkins, *God, Miracle and the Church of England*, SCM Press, 1987, p. 5.

23. P. Lapide, *The Resurrection of Jesus*, SPCK, 1984.

24. Cf. A. Jaubert, *La Date de la Cene*, Gabalda, Paris, 1955.

25. Cf. D. Daube, *The New Testament and Rabbinic Judaism*, Athlone Press, 1956, p. 310.

26. J. A. T. Robinson, 'The Shroud and the New Testament' in *Face to Face with the Turin Shroud*, ed. P. Jennings, Mayhew-McCrimmon, 1978, p. 71.

27. J. A. T. Robinson, *Redating the New Testament*, SCM Press, 1976; *The Priority of St John*, SCM Press, 1985.

28. So A. M. Farrer, *St Matthew and St Mark*, Dacre Press, 1954, p. 145, retracting his earlier agreement with R. H. Lightfoot that the gospel originally ended at Mark 16:8.

29. Cf. R. H. Lightfoot, *Locality and Doctrine in the Gospels*, Hodder, 1938, pp. 25ff.

30. C. H. Dodd, 'The appearances of the risen Christ' in *Studies in the Gospels*, ed. D. E. Nineham, OUP, 1955, pp. 9–36.

31. C. H. Dodd, *The Apostolic Preaching and its Developments*, Hodder, 1936.

32. Cf. C. F. Evans, 'The Kerygma', *Journal of Theological Studies*, new series, vol. 7, pp. 25ff.

33. For a more detailed discussion, cf. Hugh Montefiore, *Reclaiming the High Ground*, Macmillan, 1990, pp. 136ff.

34. F. Dostoevsky, *The Idiot*, Penguin, 1955, p. 419.

35. A. M. Farrer in M. C. Perry, *The Easter Enigma*, Faber, 1959, p. 11.
36. For veridical hallucinations, cf. M. C. Perry, *op. cit.*, pp. 174–87.
37. G. W. H. Lampe and D. M. Mackinnon, *The Resurrection*, Mowbray, 1966, p. 57.
38. G. K. A. Bell, *Randall Davidson*, OUP, 1930, vol. ii, p. 866.
39. *Doctrine in the Church of England*, SPCK, 1957, pp. 34f.
40. *Op. cit.*, p. 82.
41. *Ibid.*
42. *Op. cit.*, p. 84.
43. *The Nature of Christian Belief*, pp. 25f.
44. G. W. H. Lampe and D. M. Mackinnon, *op cit.*, p. 59.